Guitar Chord Songbook

Acoustic Rock

W9-CNA-691

ISBN 0-634-05061-3

HAL•LEONARD® CORPORATION

7777 W. BLUEMOUND RD. P.O. BOX 13819 MILWAUKEE, WI 53213

Visit Hal Leonard Online at
www.halleonard.com

Guitar Chord Songbook

Contents

Angie

Words and Music by Mick Jagger
and Keith Richards

Verse 1

    Am   E7
    Angie,   Angie,

G   F   C   G/B
    When will those clouds all disappear?

    Am   E7
    Angie, Angie,

G   F   C
    Where will it lead us from here?

         G
With no loving in our souls

     Dm   Am
And no money in our coats,

C   F   G
    You can't say__ we're satisfied.

    Am   E7
But Angie, Angie,

G   F   C
    You can't say we never tried.

Verse 2

Am   E7
A - Angie, you're beautiful,

G   F   C   G/B
But ain't it time we said goodbye?

Am   E7
A - Angie,   I still love ya.

G   F   C
Remember all__ those nights we cried?

G
All the dreams__ we held so close

           Dm   Am
Seemed to all__ go up in smoke.

C   F   G
Uh, let me whis-per in your ear:

  Am   E7
"Angie, Angie,

G   F   C
Where will it lead us from here?"

Bridge

    G
Oh, Angie, don't you weep.

         Dm   Am
All your kiss - es still taste sweet.

C   F   G
I hate that sadness in your eyes.

  Am   E7
But Angie, Angie,

G   F   C
Ain't it time__ we said good-bye?

           G
With no loving in our souls

         Dm   **Am**
And no money in our coats,

C   **F**   **G**
You can't say__ we're satisfied.

      Dm   **Am**
But Angie, I still love you, ba - by.

Dm   **Am**
Ev'rywhere I look I see your eyes.

Dm   **Am**
There ain't a woman that comes close to you.

C   **F**   **G**
Come on, ba - by, dry your eyes.

    Am   **E7**
But Angie, Angie,

G   **F**   **C** **G/B**
Ain't it good to be alive?

Am   **E7**
Angie, Angie,

G   **F**   **C**
They can't say we never tried.

About a Girl

Words and Music by Kurt Cobain

Tune down 1/2 step:
(low to high) E♭–A♭–D♭–G♭–B♭–E♭

E5 G C# F#7add4 A C

| Intro | ‖: **E5**　　**G**　|　**E5**　　**G**　:‖ *Play 4 times* |

Verse 1

E5 G　　**E5**　　**G**
I　　need an easy friend,

　E5 G　　**E5**　　**G**
I do,　with an ear to lend.

　E5 G　　　**E5**　　**G**
I do　think you fit this shoe,

　E5 G　　**E5**　　**G**
I do,　but you have a clue.

Chorus 1

C#　　　　**F#7add4**
　I'll take ad-vantage while

C#　　　　**F#7add4**
　You hang me out to dry,

　　E5　　　　**A C**
But I can't see you ev'ry night

　　E5 G　　**E5**　**G**
For free.

　　E5 G　　**E5**　**G**
I do.

Verse 2

E5   G   E5   G
I'm standing in your line,

E5 G   E5   G
I do, hope you have the time.

E5 G   E5   G
I do, pick a number to,

E5 G   E5   G
I do, keep a date with you.

Chorus 2

Repeat Chorus 1

Guitar Solo

Repeat Verse 1 (Instrumental)
Repeat Chorus 1 (Instrumental)

Verse 3

Repeat Verse 1

Chorus 3

C♯   F♯7add4
  I'll take ad-vantage while

C♯   F♯7add4
  You hang me out to dry,

   E5   A   C
But I can't see you ev'ry night.

E5   A   C
I can't see you ev'ry night

   E5   G   E5   G
For free.

E5   G   E5   G
I do.

E5   G   E5   G
I do.

E5   G   E5   G
I do.

E5
I do.

Across the Universe

Words and Music by
John Lennon and Paul McCartney

Melody:

Words are flow-ing out __ like end-less...

D   F#m   F#sus4   A   Aadd9   Dmaj7
132   3111   3411   111   131   111

F#m*   Em7   A7   A7*   Gm   G
134111   12 4   1 2   1 23   134111   21 3

Intro

| D | F#m F#sus4 F#m F#sus4 F#m F#sus4 F#m F#sus4 |

| A Aadd9 A Aadd9 A Aadd9 A Aadd9 |

Verse 1

D   Dmaj7   F#m*
Words are flowing out__ like endless rain into a paper cup,

     Em7   A7   A7*
They slither while they pass they slip away__ across the universe.

D   Dmaj7   F#m*
Pools of sorrow, waves of joy are drifting through my open mind,

     Em7   Gm
Pos-sessing and ca-ressing me.

Chorus 1

D   A7
Jai. Guru. Deva. Om.

Nothing's gonna change my world,

G   D
Nothing's gonna change my world.

A7
Nothing's gonna change my world,

G   D
Nothing's gonna change my world.

GUITAR CHORD SONGBOOK

Verse 2

```
        D       Dmaj7            F♯m*                          Em7
Images of broken light which dance before me like a million eyes,
                                  A7              A7*
They call me on and on across___ the universe.
        D               Dmaj7      F♯m*
Thoughts meander like a restless wind inside a letter box,
        Em7                             A7
They tumble blindly as they make their way across the universe.
```

Chorus 2   *Repeat Chorus 1*

Verse 3

```
        D               Dmaj7        F♯m*
Sounds of laughter, shades of life are ringing through my open ears,
        Em7         Gm
In-citing and in-viting me.
        D       Dmaj7        F#m*                        Em7
Limitless, un-dying love which shines around me like a million suns,
                        A7              A7*
It calls me on and on a-cross the universe.
```

Chorus 3   *Repeat Chorus 1*

Outro

```
        D
||: Jai. Guru. Deva. :||    Play 6 times and fade
```

Back to You

Words and Music by
Bryan Adams and Eliot Kennedy

Melody:

I've been down, __ I've been beat,

C	Am	F	Gsus4	G	E7	Em	Dm

Intro   ‖: C   Am | F | Gsus4| G   :‖

Verse 1
              C   **Am**
I've been down, ____ I've been beat,

         F   **Gsus4**
I've been so tired I could not speak.

      G   **C**   **Am**
I've been so lost ____ that I could not see

         F   **Gsus4**
I wanted things that were out of reach.

  G   **C**   **Am**
Then I ____ found you and you helped me through.

         F   **Gsus4**
Yeah, you showed me what to do.

    G   **F**   **E7**
And that's why ____ I'm comin' back to you, yeah.

Chorus 1

```
            Am          F                 Gsus4    G
Like a star ___ guides a ship across the o  -  cean
                      Am           F             Gsus4    G
Is how your love ___ can take me home, back to you.
                Em            Am
And if I wish ___ upon that star,
                Em              Am
Someday I'll be where you are.
              Dm                   Gsus4
And I know that day is coming soon.
                    G              C
Yeah, I'm com  -  in' back to you.
```

Interlude

```
| C     Am |       F  |      Gsus4 |
```

Verse 2

```
                G     C                 Am
You've been alone, ___ but you did not show it.
                  F                 Gsus4
You've been in pain when I did not know it.
              G     C               Am
You let me do ___ what I needed to.
                  F                 Gsus4
You were there when I needed you.
G             C                   Am
Might a let ___ you down, might a messed you around,
                F                        Gsus4
But you never changed your point of view.
                  G        F             E7
And that's why ___ I'm comin' back to you, yeah.
```

Chorus 2   *Repeat Chorus 1*

Dobro Solo   *Repeat Intro*

Verse 3

```
      G        C                    Am
Might a let ___ you down, might a messed you around,

          F                        Gsus4
But you never changed your point of view.

      G      F                 E7
And that's why ___ I'm comin' back to you, yeah.
```

Chorus 3

```
              Am        F              Gsus4   G
Like a star ___ guides a ship across the o - cean

                   Am         F          Gsus4   G
Is how your love ___ can take me home, back to you.

            Em        Am
And if I wish ___ upon that star,

          Em        Am
Someday I'll be where you are.

          Dm              Gsus4
And I know that day is coming soon.

      G                  Am
Oh,   I'm comin' back to you.
```

Outro

```
‖: Am            F │                           │
│ Gsus4           │ G                        :‖  Play 3 times
              I'm comin' back to you.

│ Am             F │                           │
│ Gsus4           │ G                           │
              That day is comin' soon.

│ Am             F │                           │
│ Gsus4           │ G                           │
              I'm comin' back to you.

│ Am             F │                           │
│ Gsus4           │ G                           │
        Yeah.

│ Am               │ F                        │ C
```

Behind Blue Eyes

Words and Music by Pete Townshend

Melody:

No one knows _ what it's like _ to be the bad man, _

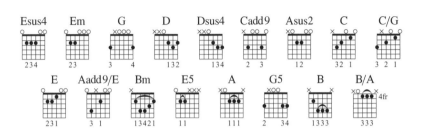

Intro

|Esus4 | | |

Verse 1

       Em   G
No one knows what it's like

            D   Dsus4 D
To be the bad man,

              Cadd9   Asus2
To be the sad man behind ____ blue eyes.

       Em   G
No one knows what it's like

           D   Dsus4 D
To be hated,

              Cadd9   Asus2
To be fated to telling on - ly lies.

Chorus 1

```
                C       D                  G     C/G  G
        But my dreams, ___ they aren't as empty
                C       D          E   Aadd9/E   E
        As my conscience seems to be.
                Bm              C
        I have hours only lone - ly.
                        D         Dsus4
        My love is ven - geance
        D           Asus2
        That's never free.
```

Verse 2

```
        Em                      G
        No one knows what it's like
                        D
        To feel these feelings
                Cadd9               Asus2
        Like I do, ___ and I blame you.
        Em                      G
        No one bites back as hard
                        D
        On their anger,
                Cadd9                   Asus2
        None of my pain and woe can show through.
```

Chorus 2   *Repeat Chorus 1*

Interlude 1 | E5   Bm | A   E5 | Bm | A   E5 |

Verse 3

```
        E5              Bm      A           E5
        When my fist clenches, crack it open

            Bm      G5      D
        Before I use it and lose my cool.

            Bm    A           D
        When I smile, tell me some bad news

            Bm    A           E5      Bm  A  E5
        Before I laugh and act like a fool.

            Bm      A       E5
        And if I swallow anything evil,

            Bm      G5      D
        Put your finger down my ___ throat.

            Bm          A           D
        And if I shiver, please ___ give me a blanket,

            Bm      A           E5
        Keep me warm, let me wear your coat.
```

Interlude 2

```
|E5    Bm|      A  E5|       Bm|      A   B|
|      A |  G5  D   B|       A |  G5  D   B|
|      A |  G5  D   B|       |B/A          |
```

Outro

```
        Em                  G
        No one knows what it's like

            D           Dsus4   D
        To be the bad man,

            Cadd9           Asus2
        To be the sad man behind ___ blue eyes.
```

Band on the Run

Words and Music by McCartney

Melody:

Stuck in - side these four   walls, ____

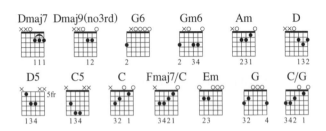

| Dmaj7 | Dmaj9(no3rd) | G6 | Gm6 | Am | D |
| 1 1 1 | 12 | 2 | 2 34 | 231 | 132 |

D5	C5	C	Fmaj7/C	Em	G	C/G
5fr						
1 3 4	1 3 4	32 1	3421	23	32 4	342 1

Intro   ‖: Dmaj7 | Dmaj9(no3rd) | G6 | :‖

| Dmaj7 | Gm6 | Dmaj7 | Gm6 |

Verse 1

Dmaj7   **Dmaj9(no3rd)**
Stuck inside these four walls,

G6
Sent inside forever.

Dmaj7   **Dmaj9(no3rd)**
Never seeing no one

G6   **Dmaj7**
Nice again like you,

Gm6 Dmaj7 Gm6 Dmaj7 Gm6
Mama, you,   Mama, you.

Interlude 1   ‖: Am | D | Am | D | Am :‖

GUITAR CHORD SONGBOOK

Verse 2

Am
If I ever get out of here,

D
Thought of giving it all away

Am
To a registered charity.

D
All I need is a pint a day.

   Am
If I ever get out of here. (If we ever get out of here.)

Interlude 2

| N.C.   ‖:D5   C5 | N.C.   :‖
| C |Fmaj7/C |C |Fmaj7/C

Verse 3

        C   Fmaj7/C
Well, the rain exploded with a mighty crash

               C
As we fell into the sun.

              Fmaj7/C
And the first one said to the second one there

            Em
I hope you're having fun.

Chorus 1

G   C
Band on the run,

Em C   Am
Band on the run.

     Fmaj7/C   C
And the jailer man and sailor Sam

    Fmaj7/C
Were searching ev'ryone.

       C   Fmaj7/C C Fmaj7/C
For the band on the run,

C   Fmaj7   C Fmaj7/C
Band on the run.

       C   Fmaj7/C C Fmaj7/C
For the band on the run,

C   Fmaj7/C C Fmaj7/C
Band on the run.

Verse 4

          C   Fmaj7/C
Well, the undertaker drew a heavy sigh

                    C
Seeing no one else had come.

                   Fmaj7/C
And a bell was ringing in the village square

                Em
For the rabbits on the run.

Chorus 2

G   C
Band on the run,

Em C   Am
Band on the run.

    Fmaj7/C   C
And the jailer man and sailor Sam

    Fmaj7/C
Were searching ev'ryone.

       C   Fmaj7/C C Fmaj7/C
For the band on the run,

C   Fmaj7/C C Fmaj7/C
Band on the run.

| Interlude 3 | `| Em  G  C/G | Em  C  Am | Fmaj7/C    |         |`
| | `| C          | Fmaj7/C    |           |         |`

```
            C    Fmaj7/C  C  Fmaj7/C
Chorus 3    Yeah, the band on the run,

             C   Fmaj7/C  C  Fmaj7/C
            The band on the run.

             C   Fmaj7/C  C  Fmaj7/C
            The band on the run,

            C    Fmaj7/C  C  Fmaj7/C
            Band on the run.
```

```
                 C                    Fmaj7/C
Verse 5     Well, the night was falling as the desert world

                             C
            Began to settle down.

                                      Fmaj7/C
            In the town they're searching for us ev'rywhere

                              Em
            But we never will be found.
```

```
            G          C
Chorus 4    Band on the run,

            Em  C      Am
            Band on the run.

                 Fmaj7/C   C
            And the county judge held a grudge;

              Fmaj7/C
            Will search forevermore

                 C    Fmaj7/C  C  Fmaj7/C
            For the band on the run,

             C    Fmaj7/C  C  Fmaj7/C
            The band on the run.

             C    Fmaj7/C  C  Fmaj7/C
            The band on the run,

             C    Fmaj7/C  C  Fmaj7/C  Em  G  C
            The band on the run.
```

Best of My Love

Words and Music by John David Souther,
Don Henley and Glenn Frey

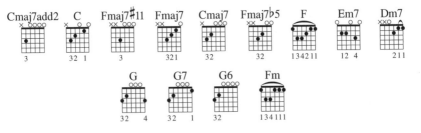

Intro   ‖: Cmaj7add2 C |Cmaj7add2   C |
            | Fmaj7#11 Fmaj7 |Fmaj7#11   Fmaj7   :‖

Verse 1

Cmaj7 C
Ev - ery night

    Cmaj7 C
I'm ly - in' in bed

Fmaj7b5 Fmaj7   Fmaj7b5 Fmaj7
Hold - in' you close in my dreams;

Cmaj7 C
Think - in' about all the things that we said

    F
And comin' apart at the seams.

Em7   Dm7
    We tried to talk it o - ver

    Em7   F
But the words come out too rough.

    Cmaj7 C
I know you were tryin'

    Fmaj7   Cmaj7 C   G G7 G6 G7
To give me the best of your love.

Verse 2

Cmaj7 C
Beau - tiful faces,

    Cmaj7 C
An' loud   empty places.

Fmaj7b5 Fmaj7   **Fmaj7b5 Fmaj7**
    Look at the way that we live,

Cmaj7 C
Wast - in' our time

On cheap talk and wine

F
    Left us so little to give.

Em7
    The same old crowd

    Dm7
Was like a cold dark cloud

        Em7   **F**
That we could never rise above,

    Cmaj7 C
But here   in my heart

 Fmaj7   **G**
I give you the best of my love.

Chorus 1

    C
Whoa,__ sweet darlin',

         F
You get the best of my love,

(You get the best of my love.)

    Cmaj7
Whoa,__ sweet darlin',

         F
You get the best of my love.

(You get the best of my love.)

Bridge

Fm
Oo, I'm goin' back in time

Cmaj7
And it's a sweet dream.

Fm
It was a quiet night

And I would be alright

Dm7   G7
If I could go on sleeping.

Cmaj7 C
Verse 3   But ev - ery morning

Cmaj7 C
I wake up and worry

Fmaj7b5 F
What's gonna happen today.

Cmaj7 C
You   see it your way,

Cmaj7 C
And I   see it mine,

F
But we both see it slippin' away.

Em7   **Dm7**
You know, we always had each other, baby.

Em7   **F**
I guess that wasn't e-nough.

Cmaj7 C
Oh, but here   in my heart

Fmaj7   **Cmaj7 C**   **G**
I give you the best of my love.

Chorus 2   ***Repeat Chorus 1 till fade***

Bridge Over Troubled Water

Words and Music by Paul Simon

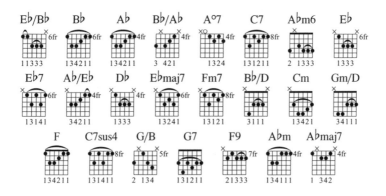

Intro

E♭/B♭ B♭	A♭ B♭/A♭ A°7	E♭/B♭ C7
A♭ A♭m6	E♭ E♭7	A♭/E♭
E♭ E♭7	A♭ E♭

Verse 1

                E♭   A♭/E♭   E♭
When you're weary,   feelin'___ small,

A♭   D♭   A♭   E♭maj7   Fm7
   When tears are in your eyes,

        E♭   A♭   E♭   A♭
I'll dry them all.

E♭   B♭/D   Cm   B♭
   I'm on   your side.

              E♭   Gm/D
Oh, when times get rough,

E♭7   A♭   F   B♭
   And friends just can't be found,

Chorus 1

E♭	B♭	A♭	B♭/A♭	A°7	E♭/B♭	C7sus4	C7

Like a bridge o - ver troubled water,

A♭	G/B	Cm

  I will lay me down.

E♭	B♭	A♭	B♭/A♭	A°7	E♭/B♭	C7sus4	C7

Like a bridge o - ver troubled water,

A♭	G/B	E♭	E♭7

  I will lay me down.

| A♭/E♭ | | E♭ | E♭7 | A♭/E♭ | | E♭ | | A♭/E♭ | |

Verse 2

        E♭

When you're down and out,

A♭/E♭		E♭

  When you're on the ___ street,

A♭	D♭	A♭	E♭maj7	Fm7

  When eve-ning falls so hard

      E♭   A♭   E♭   A♭

I will comfort you.

E♭	B♭/D	Cm	B♭

  I'll take your part.

          E♭   Gm/D

Oh, when darkness comes,

E♭7		A♭	F	B♭

  And pain is all around,

Chorus 2

E♭	B♭	A♭	B♭/A♭	A°7	E♭/B♭	C7sus4	C7

Like a bridge o - ver troubled water,

A♭	G/B	Cm

  I will lay me down.

E♭	B♭	A♭	B♭/A♭	A°7	E♭/B♭	Cm

Like a bridge o - ver troubled water,

A♭	G7	Cm	F9

  I will lay me down.

Interlude

```
|E♭/B♭   B♭    |A♭   Cm    |A♭    A♭m   |E♭        |
|A♭/E♭          |E♭   E♭7   |A♭/E♭       |E♭        |
|A♭/E♭          |
```

Verse 3

```
       E♭        A♭/E♭   E♭
Sail on silver girl,    sail on ___ by.
```
```
A♭    D♭   A♭   E♭            Fm7
  Your time has  come to shine.
```
```
         E♭                A♭       E♭        A♭
All your dreams are on their way.
```
```
E♭    B♭/D  Cm  B♭
  See how   they  shine.
```
```
         E♭      Gm/D
Oh, if you need a friend
```
```
E♭7            A♭   F    B♭
  I'm sailing right behind.
```

Chorus 3

```
E♭  B♭ A♭   B♭/A♭ A°7 E♭/B♭   Cm
Like a  bridge  o  -  ver troubled water,
```
```
A♭    G/B           Cm
  I will ease your mind.
```
```
E♭7    A♭    A♭maj7  E♭/B♭   Cm
Like a  bridge   over    troubled water,
```
```
A♭    G7           Cm           F9
  I will ease your mind.
```
```
|E♭/B♭   B♭    |A♭   Cm    |
|A♭     A♭m   |E♭   |
```

Blackbird

Words and Music by
John Lennon and Paul McCartney

Melody:

Black - bird sing-ing in the dead of night,

Intro

| G   Am7   G/B | G* |

Verse 1

G   Am7   G/B   G*
Blackbird singing in the dead of night,

C   C#°   D   D#°   Em   Em(maj7)
Take these broken wings__ and learn__ to fly.

D C#°   C   Cm
All your life,

G/B   A7   D7sus4   G
You were only wait - ing for this mo - ment to arise.

| C   G/B   A7 | D7sus4   G |

Verse 2

G   Am7   G/B   G*
Blackbird singing in the dead of night,

C   C#°   D   D#°   Em   Em(maj7)
Take these sunken eyes__ and learn__ to see.

D C#°   C   Cm
All your life,

G/B   A7   D7sus4   G
You were only wait - ing for this mo - ment to be free.

Bridge 1

F C/E   Dm C   B♭6 C
Black - bird,___ fly.

F C/E   Dm C   B♭6 A7
Black - bird,___ fly.

      D7sus4   G
Into the light_____ of a dark black night.

Interlude 1

| G Am7 G/B | G* | C C♯° D D♯° | Em Em(maj7) |
| D   C♯° | C Cm | G/B A7 | D7sus4 G |

Bridge 2

Repeat Bridge 1

Interlude 2

| G Am7 G/B | G* | | |
| G Am7 G/B C | G/B A7 D7sus4 |

Verse 3

G   Am7   G/B G*
Blackbird singing in the dead of night,

C   C♯°   D   D♯°   Em Em(maj7)
Take these broken wings__ and learn__ to fly.

D C♯° C   Cm
All your life,

G/B   A7   D7sus4   G
You were only wait - ing for this mo - ment to arise.

C   G/B A7   D7sus4   G
You were on - ly wait - ing for this mo - ment to arise.

C   G/B   A7   D7sus4   G
You were on - ly waiting__ for this mo - ment to arise.

Blowin' in the Wind

Words and Music by Bob Dylan

Melody:

How man-y roads —

(Capo 7th fret)

G   C   C/B   D/A

Intro

| G | | |

Verse 1

      G   C   C/B   D/A   G
How many roads must a man ____ walk down

               C   C/B   G
Before you call him a man?

              C   C/B   D/A   G
How many seas must a white ____ dove sail

              C   C/B   D/A
Before she sleeps in the sand?

              G   C   C/B   D/A   G
Yes, and how many times ____ must the can-nonballs fly

              C   C/B   G
Before they are for-ever banned?

Chorus 1

      C   C/B   D/A   G   C
The an-swer, my friend, is blowin' in the wind.

      C/B   D/A   G
The an-swer is blowin' in the wind.

| Interlude 1 | `| C    C/B  | D/A     | G        | C        |` |
| | `|      C/B  | D/A     | G        |          |` |

Verse 2

```
              G                 C  C/B      D/A      G
Yes, and how many years__ can a moun  -  tain exist
            C     C/B   G
Before it is washed to the sea?
                   C    C/B      D/A      G
Yes, and how many years can some people exist
              C    C/B      D/A
Before they're al-lowed to be free?
              G                C  C/B      D/A              G
Yes, and how many times ___ can a man ___ turn his head
                  C   C/B     G
And pretend that he just__ doesn't see?
```

Chorus 2   *Repeat Chorus 1*

Interlude 2   *Repeat Interlude 1*

Verse 3

```
              G      C      D/A          G
Yes, and how many   times must a man look up
                C   C/B        G
Before he can see _____ the sky?
                   C      D/A       G
Yes, and how many ears ___ must one man have
              C  C/B   D/A
Before he can hear __ people cry?
              G       C    C/B D/A          G
Yes, and how many deaths will it take till he knows
                  C        C/B   G
That too many peo - ple have died?
```

Chorus 3   *Repeat Chorus 1*

Outro   *Repeat Interlude 1*

Blue Suede Shoes

Words and Music by Carl Lee Perkins

Melody:

Well, it's one for the mon-ey,...

A   D9   E9

Verse 1

                                    A   **N.C.**   **A**
Well, it's one for the money,   two for the show,

     N.C.   **A**
Three to get ready, now go, cat, go,

     D9   **A**
But don't__ you step on my blue suede shoes.

           E9   **A**
Well, you can do anything but lay off of my blue suede shoes.

Verse 2

                     A   **N.C.**   **A**   **N.C.**   **A**
Well, you can knock me down,   step on my face,

     N.C.   **A**   **N.C.**   **A**
Slander my name all over the place.

     N.C.   **A**   **N.C.** **A**
Well, do any - thing __ that you wanna do,

     N.C.   **A**
But uh-uh, honey, lay off__ of them shoes

       D9   **A**
And don't__ you step on my blue suede shoes.

          E9   **A**
Well, you can do anything but lay off of my blue suede shoes.

Let's go cats!

Solo 1

```
| A        |          |          |          |
| D9       |     .    | A        |          |
| E9       |          | A        |          |
```

                          A   N.C.   A   N.C.   A
Verse 3   Well, you can burn my house,   steal my car,

                  N.C. A   N.C.   A
              Drink my li-quor from an old fruit jar.

                      N.C. A   N.C. A
              Well, do any-thing that you wan-na do,

              N.C.   A
              But uh-uh, honey, lay off__ of them shoes

                      D9   A
              And don't__ you step on my blue suede shoes.

                          E9   A
              Well, you can do anything but lay off of my blue suede shoes.

              Rock it!

Solo 2   *Repeat Solo 1*

Verse 4   *Repeat Verse 1*

                  A
Outro   Well, it's   blue, blue, blue suede shoes,

              Blue, blue, blue suede shoes, yeah.

              D9
                  Blue, blue, blue suede shoes, baby.

              A
                  Blue, blue, blue suede shoes.

                          E9   **A**
              Well, you can do anything but lay off of my blue suede shoes.

Catch the Wind

Words and Music by Donovan Leitch

Melody:

In the chil-ly _____ hours and

(Capo 3rd fret)

C   Fadd9   G   F   G7   Em   D/A   G6   G7*

Intro

| C | | | Fadd9 | G | |
| C | | Fadd9 | C | | |

Verse 1

          C   Fadd9   C
In the chilly hours and minutes of un-certainty

   F   C   Fadd9 G   C   G7
I want to be in the warm hold of your lovin' mind.

      C   Fadd9
To feel you all a-round me

          C   F
And to take your hand a-long the sand.

C   Fadd9 G   C   Fadd9 C
Ah, but I may as well try and catch the wind.

Verse 2

```
          C                 Fadd9
When sundown pales the sky,

          C           F
I want to hide awhile behind your smile,

C                Fadd9    G    C    G7
And ev'rywhere I'd look, your eyes I'd find.

          C           Fadd9
For me to love you now

          C           F
Would be the sweetest thing, 'twould make me sing.

C                      Fadd9 G      C      Fadd9   C
Ah, but I may as well try and catch the wind.
```

Bridge

```
F                   Em
De, de, de, de, de, de, de, de.

      F           D/A
De, de, de, de, de, de, de, de,

    G   G6   G7*   G6
De, de, de.
```

Verse 3

```
          C                 Fadd9
When rain has hung the leaves with tears,

C           F
I want you near to kill my fears,

C                Fadd9 G      C    G7
To help me to leave all my blues be-hind.

          C           Fadd9
For standing in your heart

          C           F
Is where I want to be, and long to be.

C                      Fadd9 G      C      Fadd9   C
Ah, but I may as well try and catch the wind.
```

Harp Solo   *Repeat Verse 1 (Instrumental)*

Outro

```
| C        |        | Fadd9  |        |
| C        |        | F      |        |
    C                Fadd9 G      C      Fadd9   C
Ah, but I may as well try and catch the wind.
```

Change the World

Words and Music by Wayne Kirkpatrick,
Gordon Kennedy and Tommy Sims

Melody:

If   I could reach the _ stars, _

Intro

E F#m7 Gadd9	
F#m7 E	
F#m7 Gadd9	
F#m7 Bsus4	

Verse 1

> E   A/E   E7(no 3rd)
> If I could reach the __ stars,
>
>   A/E   E
> Pull one down for you.
>
>   A/E E7(no 3rd)
> Shine it on my heart
>
>   A/E E
> So you could see the truth.
>
> A   D/A   A7(no 3rd)
> That this love I have in - side
>
>   D/A A
> Is ev'ry-thing it seems.
>
> E   A/E E7(no 3rd)
> But for now I find
>
>   A/E G#7
> It's only in my dreams.

Chorus 1

> F♯m7   G♯7   C♯m7
> And I can   change _____ the world.

> D♯m7♭5   G♯7   C♯m7
> I would be the sun - light in your universe.

> D♯m7♭5   G♯7   C♯m7   Cm7   Bm7
> You would think my love __ was really some - thin' _ good,

> A*   Eadd2/G♯
> Baby, if I could

> E/G♯   E°7/G   F♯m11
> Change _____ the world.

Interlude

E F♯m7 Gadd9		
F♯m7 E		

Verse 2

> E   A/E   E7(no3rd)
> If I could be king,

> A/E   E
> Even for a day,

> A/E   E7(no 3rd)
> I'd take you as my queen,

> A/E   E
> I'd have it no other way.

> A   D/A   A7(no 3rd)
> And our love would rule

> D/A   A
> In this kingdom we have made.

> E   A/E   E7(no 3rd)
> Till then I'd be a fool,

> A/E   G♯7
> Wishin' for the day…

Chorus 2

        F♯m7   G♯7   C♯m7
And I can   change _____ the world.

D♯m7♭5   G♯7   C♯m7
I would be the sun - light in your universe.

D♯m7♭5   G♯7   C♯m7   Cm7   Bm7
You would think my love ____ was really some - thin' __ good,

      A Eadd2/G♯
Baby, if I could

E/G♯   E°7/G   F♯m7   E   A/E
Change _____ the world.

    E   A7 Eadd2/G♯ E/G♯ E°7/G F♯m7
Ba - by, if I could   change _____ the world.

Guitar Solo

E F♯m7 Gadd9	
F♯m7 E	
F♯m7 Gadd9	
F♯m7 G♯7

Chorus 3

        F♯m7   G♯7   C♯m7
I could   change _____ the world.

D♯m7♭5   G♯7   C♯m7
I would be the sun - light in your universe.

D♯m7♭5   G♯7   C♯m7   Cm7   Bm7
You would think my love ___ was really some - thin' __ good,

      A* Eadd2/G♯   E/G♯   E°7/G   F♯m11
Baby, if I could   change the __ world,

      A* Eadd2/G♯   E/G♯   E°7/G   F♯m11
Baby, if I could   change the __ world,

      A* Eadd2/G♯   E/G♯   E°7/G   Gadd9
Baby, if I could   change _____ the world.

Outro

| E F♯m7 Gadd9 | | F♯m7 | E

Could You Be Loved

Words and Music by Bob Marley

Melody:

Could you be loved?

D   G   Bm   Em   F♯m   Em*   A

Intro

‖: **N.C.(Bm)** :‖ *Play 6 times*

Chorus 1

D
Could you be loved?

G   **D**
Then be loved.

Could you be loved?

G   **D**
Then be loved.

Verse 1

Bm   **Em**
Don't let them fool ya,

Bm   **Em**
Or even try to school ya.

Oh, no.

Bm
We've got a mind of our own.

        G   **F♯m**   **Em***
So, go to hell if what   you thinkin' is not right.

Bm
Love would never leave us alone.

        G   **F♯m**   **A**
Ah, in the darkness, there must come out to light.

	D Bm
Chorus 2	Could you be loved?

G   D
Then be loved.

                              Bm
Now, could you be loved?

              G
Whoa,__ yeah.

                      D   Bm
Then be loved.

	Bm
Verse 2	*Could you be loved, now, could you be loved?*

The road of life is rocky and you may stumble too.

So, why don't you point your fingers at someone else that's judging you.

(Could you be, could you be, could you be loved?)

(Could you be, could you be loved?)

(Could you be, could you be, could you be loved?)

(Could you be, could you be loved?)

Verse 3

Bm   Em
    Don't let them change ya, oh,

Bm
    Or even rearrange ya.

Em
    Oh, no.

Bm
    We've got the life to live.

 G   F♯m Em*
(Ooh, ooh, ooh.)

          Bm
They say   only, only,

         G   F♯m   A
Only the fittest of the fittest shall survive.

Stay alive. Eh.

Chorus 3

D   Bm
    Could you be loved?

G   D
    Then be loved.

                   Bm
Now, could you be loved?

        G   D
Whoa, __ yeah. Then be loved.

Outro

Bm
(Ain't gonna miss the water until the well runs dry.)

(And no matter how you treat the man, he'll never be satisfied.)

‖: Say something. Say something. :‖ *Repeat and fade*
(w/ voc. ad lib.)

Come to My Window

Words and Music by Melissa Etheridge

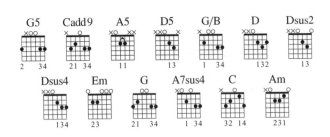

Intro

G5   **Cadd9**   **A5**   **D5**
Come to my win - dow.

G5   **Cadd9**   **A5**   **D5**   **G5**
Crawl in-side, wait ____ by the light ____ of the moon.

     Cadd9   **A5**
Come to my win - dow,

D5
I'll be home soon.

Cadd9 G/B		D Dsus2 D Dsus2	Cadd9 G/B	
Dsus2 D Dsus2 Dsus2	Cadd9 G/B	
D Dsus2 D Dsus2	Cadd9 G/B	D Dsus2

Verse 1

```
Cadd9        G/B
I would dial the numbers

        D                    Dsus4  D  Dsus2
Just to lis - ten to your breath.

        Cadd9        G/B
And I would stand in-side my hell

        D                Dsus2  D  Dsus2
And hold ___ the hand of death.

Cadd9            G/B
You don't know how far I'd go

D                    Dsus4  D  Dsus2
To ease this precious ache.

        Cadd9            G/B
And you don't know how much I'd give

D
Or how much I can take.
```

Pre-Chorus 1

```
            Em        Cadd9
Just to reach ___ you.

            D
Just to reach ___ you.

Dsus4  D    Em              Cadd9  D  Dsus2  D   Dsus2
Oh, ___ to ___ reach you, _____ oh.
```

Chorus 1

```
G      Cadd9  A7sus4      D  Dsus2  D  Dsus2
Come to my win  -  dow.

G          Cadd9
Crawl in-side,

    A7sus4          D    Dsus2  D  Dsus2
Wait ___ by the light ___ of ___ the__ moon.

G      Cadd9  A7sus4
Come to my win  -  dow,

    D  Dsus2    D Dsus2 G   Cadd9  A7sus4  D  Dsus2  D  Dsus2
I'll ___ be__ home _____ soon.
```

Verse 2

Cadd9   G/B
Keeping my eyes open

        Dsus4 Dsus2 D Dsus4   D Dsus2
I cannot ____ af - ford to ____ sleep.

Cadd9   G/B
Giving away promises

        D   Dsus4   D Dsus2
I know __ that I can't ____ keep.

Cadd9   G/B
Nothing fills the blackness

          Dsus2 D Dsus2 Dsus4 D Dsus2
That has seeped _____ into my   chest.

 Cadd9   G/B
I need you in my ___ blood

        D   Dsus4 D Dsus4 D
I am forsak - ing all the rest.

Pre-Chorus 2   *Repeat Pre-Chorus 1*

          G   Cadd9 A7sus4   D Dsus2 D Dsus2

Chorus 2
         Come to my win - dow.

          G   Cadd9
         Crawl in-side,

         A7sus4   D   Dsus2 D Dsus2
Wait ____ by the light __ of ____ the__ moon.

          G   Cadd9 A7sus4
         Come to my win - dow,

         D Dsus2   D Dsus2 G   Cadd9   A7sus4 D
I'll __ be___ home _____ soon.

Bridge

Em
I don't care what they think.

C
I don't care what they say.

Am
What do they know about this love,

D   Dsus4 D   Dsus2   Dsus4   D
Any - way?

Interlude

|G   Cadd9 |A7sus4 Dsus4 D Dsus2 D Dsus2|
|G   Cadd9 |A7sus4   Dsus4 |

       Cadd9   G/B   D   Dsus2 D
Come, ____ come __ to my win-dow,

Dsus4 D Dsus2   Cadd9
I'll   be home, I'll ____ be home,

  G/B   D   Dsus2
I'll ___ be home.   I'm comin' home.

Chorus 3

G   Cadd9   A7sus4
Come to my win - dow.

D Dsus2 D G   Cadd9
Oh, _____   crawl in-side,

  A7sus4   D   Dsus2 D   G
Wait ___ by the light ___ of the ___ moon.

       Cadd9   A7sus4
Come to my win - dow,

  D   Dsus2   G
I'll ___ be home soon,

  Cadd9   A7sus4
I'll ___ be home, I'll____ be home,

  D   Dsus2
I'm comin' home.

Chorus 4   *Repeat Chorus 3*

Outro   ‖: G   Cadd9 | A7sus4   D Dsus2 :‖ *Repeat and fade*

COUSTIC ROCK   **45**

Crazy Little Thing Called Love

Words and Music by Freddie Mercury

Verse 1

            D
This thing__ called love,

      G   **C**   **G**
I just__ can't handle it.

           D
This thing,__ called love,

      G   **C**   **G**
I must__ get 'round to it.

        D
I ain't ready.

Bb   **C**   **D**
Crazy little thing called love.

Verse 2

           D
This thing__ (This thing.) called love, (Called love.)

      G   **C**   **G**
It cries__ (Like a baby.) in a cradle all night.

         D
It swings,__ (Woo, woo.) it jives, (Woo,woo.)

      G   **C**   **G**
It shakes__ all over like a jellyfish.

        D
I kinda like it.

Bb   **C**   **D**
Crazy little thing called love.

Bridge 1
             G7
There goes my baby,

    C   **G**
She knows how to rock 'n' roll.

       Bb
She drives me crazy.

      E   **A**
She gives me hot and cold fever,

     F   **N.C.** **E**
Then she leaves me in a cool, cool sweat.

    A   **D**
Verse 3   I gotta be cool,__ relax,

    G **C** **G**
Get hip,__ get on my tracks,

    D
Take the back seat, hitch hike,

  G   **C** **G**
And take a long ride on my motor-bike

    D
Until I'm ready.

Bb   **C**   **D**
Crazy little thing called love.

Bridge 2   ***Repeat Bridge 1***

Verse 4   ***Repeat Verse 3***

Verse 5   ***Repeat Verse 1***

       Bb   **C**   **D**
Outro ‖: Crazy little thing called love. :‖ ***Repeat and fade***

Daydream

Words and Music by John Sebastian

Melody:

What a day for a day - dream,

(Capo 1st fret)

C   A7   Dm7   G   F   D7/F♯   C/G

Intro

| C | | | |

Verse 1

C   A7
What a day for a day - dream,
Dm7   G
What a day for a daydreamin' boy.
C   A7
And I'm lost in a day - dream,
Dm7   G
Dreamin' 'bout my bundle of joy.

Bridge 1

F   D7/F♯   C/G   A7
And even if time ain't really on my side,
F   D7/F♯   C/G   A7
It's one of those days for taking a walk outside.
F   D7/F♯   C/G   A7
I'm blowing the day to take a walk in the sun,
G
And fall on my face on somebody's new mown lawn.

Verse 2

C   A7
I've been having a sweet ___ dream,
Dm7   G
I've been dreamin' since I woke up today.
C   A7
It's starring me and my sweet ___ dream,
Dm7   G
'Cause she's the one makes me feel this way.

Bridge 2

```
         F            D7/F#      C/G    A7
         And even if time is passing by a lot,

         F              D7/F#       C/G          A7
         I couldn't care less about the dues you say I ___ got.

         F              D7/F#         C/G                 A7
         Tomorrow I'll pay the dues for dropping my load,

         G
         A pie in the face for being a sleepy bull toad.
```

Interlude

‖: C | A7 | Dm7 | G   :‖

Verse 3

```
         F                    D7/F#        C/G      A7
         And you can be sure that if you're feelin' right,

         F            D7/F#   C/G      A7
         A daydream will last till long into the night.

         F          D7/F#           C/G             A7
         Tomorrow at breakfast you may pick up your ears,

         G
         Or you may be daydreamin' for a thousand years.
```

Verse 4

```
         C                   A7
         What a day for a day - dream,

         Dm7            G
         Custom made for a daydreamin' boy.

         C                   A7
         Now, I'm lost in a day - dream,

         Dm7           G
         Dreamin' 'bout my bundle of joy.
```

Outro

‖: F   D7/F# | C/G   A7 :‖ *Repeat and fade*

Don't Stop

Words and Music by Christine McVie

If you wake up and don't want to smile; —

E	A/E	D	A	B	D/E
231	234	132	123	1333	1131

Intro   ‖: E A/E │ E A/E │ E A/E │ E A/E :‖

Verse 1

    E   D   A
If you wake up and don't want to smile;

    E   D   A
If it takes just a little while,

    E   D   A
Open your eyes and look at the day.

    B
You'll see things in a diff'rent way.

Chorus 1

    E   D/E A
Don't stop   thinking about tomorrow.

    E   D/E A
Don't stop.   It'll soon be here.

    E   D/E A
It'll be _____ better than before.

    B
Yesterday's gone. Yesterday's gone.

Interlude   │E   D │A   │E   D │A   │

Verse 2

```
         E        D      A
         Why not think about times to come,

         E          D      A
         And not a-bout the things that you've done.

         E       D      A
         If your life was bad to you,

         B
         Just think what tomorrow will do.
```

Chorus 2   *Repeat Chorus 1*

Guitar Solo |E   D |A |E   D |A |
               |E   D |A |B | |
               | | | |

Verse 3

```
         E       D       A
         All I want is to see you smile,

         E    D        A
         If it takes just a little while.

         E            D       A
         I know you don't be-lieve that it's true.

         B
         I never meant any harm to you.
```

Chorus 3

```
         E    D/E   A
         Don't stop   thinking about tomorrow.

         E     D/E    A N.C.
         Don't stop.  It'll soon be here.

         E       D/E   A
         It'll be _____ better than before.

         B
         Yesterday's gone. Yesterday's gone.
```

Chorus 4   *Repeat Chorus 1*

Outro

```
         E    D/E  A              E     D/E   A
      ‖: Ooh, _____ don't you look back.        :‖ Repeat and fade
```

Drive

Words and Music by Brandon Boyd,
Michael Einziger, Alex Katunich,
Jose Pasillas II and Chris Kilmore

Melody:

Some-times   I   feel _ the fear _ of ____

Em   Em9   Cmaj7   A7sus2   A7   A7sus2*

Intro   ‖: Em   Em9 | Cmaj7   A7sus2 :‖ *Play 4 times*

Verse 1
   Em   Em9 Cmaj7 A7sus2
   Sometimes I feel the fear of

    Em   Em9 Cmaj7 A7sus2
    Un-certainty stinging clear.

   Em Em9 Cmaj7
   And I, I can't help but ask myself

   A7sus2   Em   Em9 Cmaj7 A7sus2
   How much I'll let the fear take the wheel ____ and steer.

Pre-Chorus 1
   Cmaj7   A7
   It's driven me be-fore,

       A7sus2* A7 A7sus2* Cmaj7
   And it seems to have ____ a vague,

   A7   A7sus2* A7 A7sus2* Cmaj7
   Haunting mass ap - peal.

       A7   A7sus2* A7
   But lately I'm beginning to   find ____ that

   A7sus2* Cmaj7   A7
   I _____ should be the one behind the wheel.

Chorus 1

Em   Em9 Cmaj7   A7sus2 Em

Whatever tomor - row brings, I'll be ___ there

Em9   Cmaj7   A7sus2

With open arms ___ and open eyes, ___ yeah.

Em   Em9 Cmaj7   A7sus2 Em

Whatever tomor - row brings, I'll be ___ there,

Em9 Cmaj7 A7sus2

I'll be ___ there.

Verse 2

Em   Em9   Cmaj7   A7sus2

So if I   de-cide to waiver my

Em   Em9 Cmaj7 A7sus2

Chance to be one of the hive,

Em   Em9   Cmaj7   A7sus2

Will I   choose water over wine

Em

And hold my own and drive?

Em9 Cmaj7 A7sus2

Oh, oh, oh.

Pre-Chorus 2

Cmaj7   A7

It's driven me be-fore,

A7sus2* A7 A7sus2* Cmaj7

And it seems to have ___ a vague,

A7   A7sus2* A7 A7sus2* Cmaj7

Haunting mass ap -   peal.

A7   A7sus2* A7

But lately I'm beginning to find ___

A7sus2* Cmaj7   A7

That when _____ I drive my-self my light is found.

Chorus 2	*Repeat Chorus 1*
Interlude	*Repeat Intro*

Pre-Chorus 3

Cmaj7   A7   Cmaj7
Would you choose a, water over wine?

A7   N.C.
Hold the wheel and drive.

Chorus 3   *Repeat Chorus 1*

Outro

Em   Em9   Cmaj7   A7sus2
    Do, do, do, ____ do, do, do,

          Em
Do, do, do, ____ do.

Em9   Cmaj7
No, no, ____ no.

   A7sus2   Em
Do, do, do, do, do.

     Em9   Cmaj7   A7sus2
Do, do, do, do, ____ do, do, do,

          Em
Do, do, do, ____ do.

Em9 Cmaj7   A7sus2   Cmaj7   A7
No, no, __ no, no, no.

Fast Car

Words and Music by Tracy Chapman

Melody:

You got a fast ___ car,

(Capo 2nd fret)

Cmaj7 G Em Dadd4 C D

Intro

‖: Cmaj7   G |Em   Dadd4   :‖ *Play 4 times*

Verse 1

Cmaj7   G
You got a fast ___ car,

Em   Dadd4
I want a ticket ____ to anywhere.

Cmaj7   G
Maybe we make a deal,

Em   Dadd4
Maybe together we can get somewhere.

Cmaj7   G
Anyplace is better.

Em   Dadd4
Starting from zero, got nothing to lose.

Cmaj7   G
Maybe we'll make something;

Em   Dadd4
Me, myself, I got nothing to prove.

Interlude 1   ‖: Cmaj7   G |Em   Dadd4   :‖

Verse 2

Cmaj7   G
You got a fast __ car,

Em   Dadd4
I got a plan ____ to get us out of here.

        Cmaj7   G
I been working at the con-venience store,

Em   Dadd4
Managed to save just a little bit of money.

Cmaj7   G
Won't have to drive too far,

        Em   Dadd4
Just 'cross the border and into the city.

Cmaj7   G
You and I can both get jobs

        Em   Dadd4
And finally see what it means to be living.

Interlude 2   *Repeat Interlude 1*

Verse 3

        Cmaj7   G
You see, my old man's got a problem.

    Em   Dadd4
He live with the bottle, that's the way it is.

        Cmaj7   G
He says his body's too old for working;

    Em   Dadd4
His body's too young ____ to look like his.

    Cmaj7   G
My mama went off and left him;

        Em   Dadd4
She wanted more from life than he could give.

        Cmaj7   G
I said somebody's got to take care of him.

        Em   Dadd4
So I quit school and that's what I did.

Interlude 3   *Repeat Interlude 1*

Verse 4
```
Cmaj7       G
```
You got a fast __ car,
```
        Em          Dadd4
```
But is it fast enough so we can fly away?
```
Cmaj7       G
```
We gotta make a decision:
```
Em             Dadd4
```
Leave tonight or live and die this way.
```
|Cmaj7   G   |Em   Dadd4  |Cmaj7   G      |
Em      Dadd4
```
   'Cause I remember when we were...

Chorus 1
```
C
```
Driving, driving in your car,
```
     G
```
The speed so fast I felt like I was drunk.
```
Em
```
   City lights lay out before us
```
          D
```
And your arm felt nice wrapped 'round my shoulder.
```
     C   Em    D
```
And I, I had a feeling that I belonged.
```
C  Em     D
```
I, I had a feeling I could be someone,
```
C          D
```
Be someone, be someone.

Interlude 4   *Repeat Interlude 1*

Verse 5

      Cmaj7   **G**
You got a fast __ car.

Em   **Dadd4**
We go cruising to entertain ourselves.

      Cmaj7   **G**
You still ain't got a job

      Em   **Dadd4**
And I work in a market as a checkout girl.

Cmaj7   **G**
I know things will get better;

Em   **Dadd4**
You'll find work and I'll get promoted.

Cmaj7   **G**
We'll move out of the shelter,

Em   **Dadd4**
Buy a big house and live in the suburbs.

| **Cmaj7** **G** | **Em** **Dadd4** | **Cmaj7** **G** | |

Em   **Dadd4**
  'Cause I remember when we were...

Chorus 2   *Repeat Chorus 1*

Interlude 5   *Repeat Interlude 1*

Verse 6

```
Cmaj7      G
You got a fast __ car.

Em          Dadd4
I got a job that pays all our bills.

   Cmaj7        G
You stay out drinking   late at the bar;

   Em                  Dadd4
See more of your friends than you do of your kids.

Cmaj7        G
I'd always hoped for better;

      Em           Dadd4
Thought maybe together    you and me'd find it.

   Cmaj7      G
I got no plans, I ain't going nowhere,

   Em              Dadd4
So take your fast car and keep on driving.
```
| Cmaj7   G | Em   Dadd4 | Cmaj7   G |
```
Em      Dadd4
   'Cause I remember when we were...
```

Chorus 3   *Repeat Chorus 1*

Interlude 6   *Repeat Interlude 1*

Verse 7

```
Cmaj7      G
You got a fast __ car.

   Em          Dadd4
Is it fast enough so you can fly away?

Cmaj7        G
You gotta make a decision:

Em          Dadd4
Leave tonight or live and die this way.
```

Outro

‖: Cmaj7   G | Em   Dadd4   :‖ *Play 3 times*
| Cmaj7   G

Dust in the Wind

Words and Music by Kerry Livgren

Melody:

I close my eyes,

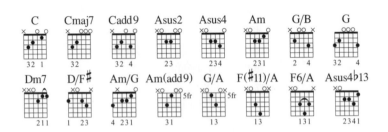

C   Cmaj7   Cadd9   Asus2   Asus4   Am   G/B   G

Dm7   D/F♯   Am/G   Am(add9)   G/A   F(♯11)/A   F6/A   Asus4♭13

Intro

C Cmaj7	Cadd9 C	Asus2 Asus4
Am Asus2	Cadd9 C	Cmaj7 Cadd9
Am Asus2	Asus4 Am G/B

Verse 1

  C   G/B   Am
I close my   eyes,

G   Dm7   Am   G/B
Only for a mo - ment, and the mo - ment's gone.

C   G/B Am
All   my   dreams

G   Dm7   Am
Pass before my eyes, ___ a curi-osity.

Chorus 1

D/F♯   G   Am   Am/G
  Dust ___ in the wind.

D/F♯   G   Am   G/B
All they are is dust in the wind.

Verse 2

```
C    G/B Am
Same old  song.

G              Dm7          Am
Just a drop of wa - ter in an end - less sea.

C  G/B Am
All  we  do

G                   Dm7            Am
Crumbles to the ground __ though we re-fuse to see.
```

Chorus 2

```
D/F♯   G     Am  Am/G
  Dust __in the wind.

D/F♯      G        Am(add9)   G/A
All we are is dust in the wind.

F(♯11)/A  F6/A  F(♯11)/A
Oh, ho,    ho.
```

Interlude 1   ‖: Am(add9) | G/A | F(♯11)/A | F6/A F(♯11)/A :‖

Interlude 2   *Repeat Intro*

Verse 3

```
G/B C   G/B Am
Now don't hang on,

G              Dm7           Am
Nothing lasts forev - er but the earth __ and sky.

G/B C   G/B Am
It   slips  a - way

    G              Dm7          Am
And all your money won't another minute buy.
```

Chorus 3

```
D/F♯   G     Am  Am/G
  Dust __ in the wind.

D/F♯      G            Am  Am/G
All we are is dust in the wind.

D/F♯  G     Am     Am/G
  Dust __ in the wind.

D/F♯      G         Am
Ev'rything is dust in the wind.
```

Outro   ‖: Am Asus2 | Asus4♭13 Am | Asus2 Asus4♭13 :‖ *Repeat and fade*

Fields of Gold

Music and Lyrics by Sting

Melody:

You'll re - mem - ber me

Bm7   G   D   G/B   Asus4   Gsus2

Intro   ‖: Bm7 | :‖ *Play 4 times*

Verse 1
                Bm7   **G**
You'll re-member me when the west wind moves
                     D
Upon the fields of bar - ley.
                Bm7   **G**   **D**
You'll for-get the sun in his jealous sky
            G/B   **Asus4** **D**
As we walk in fields of gold.
   |**Bm7** | **Gsus2**|**D** |
           Bm7   **G**
So she took her love for to gaze a while
                     D
Upon the fields of bar - ley.
         Bm7   **G**   **D**
In his arms she fell as her hair came down
          G/B   **Asus4** **D**
Among ___ the fields of gold.

Verse 2

Bm7   G
Will you stay with me, will you be my love

              D
Among the fields of bar - ley?

    Bm7   G   D
We'll for-get the sun in his jealous sky

  G/B Asus4 D
As we lie in fields of gold.

| Bm7 | | Gsus2 | D | | |

    Bm7   G
See the west wind move like a lover so

              D
Upon the fields of bar - ley.

    Bm7   G   D
Feel her body rise when you kiss her mouth

  G/B   Asus4 D
Among ___ the fields of gold.

Bridge

Gsus2   D
I never made promises lightly

Gsus2   D
And there have been some that I've broken,

Gsus2   D
But I swear in the days still left

    G/B   Asus4 D
We'll walk ___ in fields of gold.

    G/B   Asus4 D
We'll walk in fields of gold.

| *Guitar Solo* | | Bm7 | | G | | | | D | | |
| | | Bm7 | | G | D | | G/B Asus4 | D | | |

Verse 3

      Bm7   **G**
Many years have passed since those __ summer days

                 D
Among the fields of bar - ley.

      Bm7   **G**   **D**
See the children run as the sun goes down

     G/B   **Asus4** **D**
Among ____ the fields of gold.

       Bm7   **G**
You'll re-member me when the west wind moves

                D
Upon the fields of bar - ley.

       Bm7   **G**   **D**
You can tell the sun in his jealous sky

D   **G/B**   **Asus4** **D**
When we walked in fields of gold.

        G/B   **Asus4** **D**
When we walked in fields of gold,

        G/B   **Asus4** **D**
When we walked in fields of gold.

Outro   ‖: **D**   **Gsus2** **D** :‖ *Play 7 times*
                 | **D**

Iris
from the Motion Picture CITY OF ANGELS

Words and Music by John Rzeznik

Tuning:
(low to high) B-D-D-D-D-D

Intro ‖: D5   Dmaj7/C# | D5 D5* | Gmaj7   Dadd9/F# D5* :‖

Verse 1

       D5**   E7   G5
And I'd give up forev - er to touch__ you

         Bm   Asus4   G5
'Cause I know__ that you feel__ me some-how.

         D5**   E7   G5
You're the clos - est to heav - en that I'll__ ever be,

         Bm   Asus4   G5
And I don't__ wanna go__ home right now.

         D5**   E7   G5
And all__ I could taste__ is this moment,

       Bm   Asus4   G5
And all__ I can breathe__ is your life.

       D5**   E7   G5
Well, sooner or lat - er it's o - ver.

        Bm   Asus4   G5
I just don't__ wanna miss__ you tonight.

ACOUSTIC ROCK

Chorus 1

        Bm   **Asus4**   **G5**

And I don't want the world__ to see__ me

            Bm   **Asus4**   **G5**

'Cause I don't__ think that they'd__ under-stand.

    Bm   **Asus4**   **G5**

When everything's made to be bro - ken

         Bm   **Asus4** **G5**

I just want__ you to know__ who I am.

Interlude 1   *Repeat Intro*

Verse 2

          D5**   **E7**   **G5**

And you can't__ fight the tears__ that ain't comin',

     Bm   **Asus4**   **G5**

Or the mo - ment of truth__ in your lies.

   D5**   **E7**   **G5**

When ev'rything feels like the mov - ies,

         Bm   **Asus4**   **G5**

Yeah, you bleed__ just to know__ you're alive.

Chorus 2   *Repeat Chorus 1*

```
Interlude 2   ‖: Bm  Dmaj7/C#* | D5*** | Bm    Asus4 |G5      :‖
              ‖: Bm  Dmaj7/C#*  D5*** |G5            :‖   Play 4 times
               | D/F#     | G5      |Bm        | G5       |
               | D/F#     | Bm      |
               |   Dmaj7/C#* D5*** E7* D5*** Dmaj7/C#*   |
               | G5       | D/F#    |Bm        |          |
              ‖: Bm  Dmaj7/C#* |D5***  | Bm Asus4 |G5      :‖
```

Chorus 3   *Repeat Chorus 1*

Chorus 4   *Repeat Chorus 1*


```
                    Bm              Asus4    G5
Outro         I just want__ you to know__ who I am.

                    Bm              Asus4    G5
              I just want__ you to know__ who I am.

                    Bm              Asus4    G5
              I just want__ you to know__ who I am.

                    Bm              Asus4    Bm
              I just want__ you to know__ who I am.
              ‖:Bm  Dmaj7/C#* | D5*** |Bm Asus4 |G5 :‖   Repeat and fade
```

Give a Little Bit

Words and Music by Rick Davies
and Roger Hodgson

D	G	A	Bm	E7	Bm/A	F#7	Gmaj7	C
132	21 34	123	13421	2 1	3421	131211	1 342	32 1

Verse 1

  D
  Give a little bit,

      G   **A**   **G A** **G**
Give a little bit of your love__ to me.

  D   **A**
  I'll give a little bit,

  D   **G** **A**   **G A** **G**
  I'll give a little bit of my love__ to you.

Bm   **E7**
  There's so much that we need__ to share,

  G   **Bm/A** **A**   **D** **A**
So send a smile and show__ you care.

Verse 2

  D   **A**
  I'll give a little bit,

  D   **G** **A**   **G** **A** **G**
  I'll give a little bit of my life__ for you.

  D   **A**
  So, give a little bit,

  D   **G**   **A**   **G** **A** **G**
  Oh, give a little bit of your time__ to me.

Bm   **E7**
  See the man with the lone - ly eyes?

  G   **Bm/A** **A**   **D** **A**
Oh, take his hand, you'll be sur - prised.

Solo   ‖: F#7 | Gmaj7   :‖
           | C G | A D | A | D | A |

            D
Verse 3   Give a little bit,

                    G   A   G A   G
    Give a little bit of your love___ to me.

    D   A
     I'll give a little bit,

    D   G   A   G A   G
     I'll give a little bit of my life___ to you.

    Bm   E7
     Now's the time that we need___ to share,

      G
    So find yourself,

         C   G   A   D
    We're on our way back home.

    A   D   A   D
     Oh,___ goin' home.

    A   D   A   D
     Don't you need, don't you need to feel at home?

    A   D   G A   G   D
     Oh, yeah,___ we gotta sing.

Have You Ever Really Loved a Woman?
from the Motion Picture DON JUAN DeMARCO

Words and Music by Bryan Adams,
Michael Kamen and Robert John Lange

Melody:

To real - ly ___ love a wom - an,

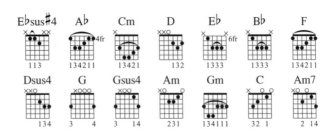

Ebsus#4	Ab	Cm	D	Eb	Bb	F
113	134211 4fr	13421	132	1333 6fr	1333	134211

Dsus4	G	Gsus4	Am	Gm	C	Am7
134	3	4	3 14	231	134111	32 1	2 14

Intro |Ebsus#4 |Ab   Cm |D |

Verse 1

                                         Eb
To really love a wom - an,

              Cm
To under-stand her

           D
You got to know her deep inside.

             Bb
Hear ev'ry thought, see ev'ry dream

             F
And give her wings when she wants to fly.

             Cm
Then when you find yourself

                   Dsus4   D
Lying helpless in her arms.

Chorus 1

      G   D   Gsus4 G
You know you really love a woman.

                                            D
When you love a woman you tell her she's really want - ed.

                                      G
When you love a woman you tell her that she's the one.

'Cause she needs somebody to tell her

                       Am D   Am   D
That it's gonna last_____ for-ever.

      Am   D
So tell me have you ever really,

Am   D   G
Really, really ever loved a woman? Yeah.

Verse 2

                Gm
To really love a woman,

           Cm
Let her hold you

        D
Till you know how she needs to be touched.

           B♭   Am
You got to breathe her, really taste her

Gm   F
  Till you can feel her in your blood.

           E♭
And when you can see

                  Dsus4 D
Your unborn children in her eyes.

Chorus 2

     E♭   **D** **Gsus4** **G**

You know you really love a woman.

When you love a woman

          D

You tell her she's really want - ed. Yeah.

When you love a woman

          G

You tell her that she's the one.

'Cause she needs somebody to tell her

       Am **D**   **Am** **D**

That you'll always be _____ togeth - er.

  Am   **D**

So tell me have you ever really,

Am   **D**   **G**

Really, really ever loved a woman?

         E♭

Bridge

Oh, you've got to give her some faith,

         G

Hold her tight, a little tenderness,

You got to treat her right.

D

She will be there for you;

         G

Taking good care of you.

You really got to love your woman, yeah.

Guitar Solo

```
| E♭        | Cm       | D        |          B♭  F |
| B♭        | F    Am  | F        |                |
```

Interlude

                      Cm
        And when you find yourself

                          Dsus4   D
        Lying helpless in her arms

                          Gsus4   G
        You know you really love a wom-an.

Chorus 3

                      G
        When you love a woman

                                    D
        You tell her that she's really want - ed.

        When you love a woman

                              G
        You tell her that she's the one. Yeah.

        'Cause she needs somebody to tell her

                          Am   D   Am   D
        That it's gonna last _____ for-ever.

            Am   D
        So tell me have you ever really,

        Am   D   G
        Really, really ever loved a woman? Yeah.

              C   D
        Just tell me have you ever really,

        C   D   G
        Really, really ever loved a woman?

                  C   D
        Oh, just tell me have you ever really,

        Am7   D   G
        Really, really ever loved a woman?

Here Comes the Sun

Words and Music by George Harrison

Melody:

Here comes_ the sun, ___

(Capo 7th fret)

Intro	‖: D | |G |A7 :‖	

Chorus 1

  D   Dsus2 D
  Here comes the sun,

  G   E7
  Here comes the sun,

      D   Dsus2 D
And I say it's all   right.
|Bm(add11) Asus4 |G6 Asus4 A7 |

Verse 1

  D   Dsus2 D   G   A7 A7sus4
  Little dar - ling, it's been a long, cold, lonely win - ter.

  D   Dsus2 D   G   A7 A7sus4
  Little dar - ling, it feels like years since it's been here.

Chorus 2

  D   Dsus2 D
  Here comes the sun,

  G   E7
  Here comes the sun,

      D   Dsus2 D
And I say it's all   right.
|Bm(add11) Asus4 |G6 Asus4 A7 |D |A7 |

Verse 2

```
D       Dsus2 D                  G                 A7  A7sus4
Little dar  -  ling, the smile's re-turning to their faces,

D       Dsus2 D                  G                     A7  A7sus4
Little dar  -  ling, it seems like years since it's been here.
```

Chorus 3   *Repeat Chorus 2*

Bridge

```
|F    |C    |G/B  |G    |D    |A7   |
||: F    |C    |G/B  |G    |D    |A7  :||  Play 5 times
  Sun,  sun,   sun,   here it comes.
|A7   |A7sus4 |A7   |A7sus4  A   |
```

Verse 3

```
D       Dsus2 D                  G              A7   A7sus4
Little dar  -  ling, I feel that ice is slowly melt - ing.

D       Dsus2 D                  G                     A7  A7sus4
Little dar  -  ling, it seems like years since it's been clear.
```

Chorus 4   *Repeat Chorus 1*

Chorus 5

```
D       Dsus2 D
Here comes the sun,

G                 E7
Here comes the sun,

D
It's alright.

|Bm(add11) Asus4   |G6  Asus4 A7 |

D
It's all right.

|Bm(add11) Asus4   |G6  Asus4 A7 |
|F    C  |G/B  G  |D/A  |
```

Here, There and Everywhere

Words and Music by
John Lennon and
Paul McCartney

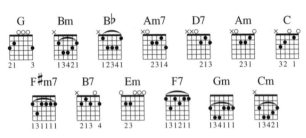

Intro

    G   **Bm**
    To lead a better life,

    B♭   **Am7** **D7**
    I need my love to be here.

Verse 1

    G   **Am**
    Here,

    Bm   **C**   **G** **Am**
    Making each day__ of the year.

    Bm   **C**   **F♯m7**   **B7**
    Changing my life__ with a wave__ of her hand.

    F♯m7   **B7**   **Em**   **Am**   **Am7** **D7**
    Nobody can__ deny__ that there's some - thing there.

Verse 2

    G   **Am**
    There,

    Bm   **C**   **G** **Am**
    Running my hands__ through her hair.

    Bm   **C**   **F♯m7**   **B7**
    Both of us think - ing how good__ it can be.

    F♯m7   **B7**   **Em**   **Am**   **Am7** **D7**
    Someone is speak-ing, but she doesn't know__ he's there.

Bridge 1
```
      F7      Bb        Gm
I want her ev'rywhere,

        Cm           D7          Gm
And if she's beside me, I know I need never care.

Cm          D7
But to love her is to need her
```

Verse 3
```
      G           Am
Ev'rywhere.

Bm              C           G   Am
Knowing that love__ is to share.

Bm              C           F#m7        B7
Each one believ - ing that love__ never dies,

F#m7               B7    Em          Am        Am7  D7
Watching their eyes__ and hoping I'm al - ways there.
```

Bridge 2
```
      F7      Bb        Gm
I want her ev'rywhere,

        Cm           D7          Gm
And if she's beside me, I know I need never care.

Cm          D7
But to love her is to need her
```

Verse 4
```
G           Am
Ev'rywhere.

Bm              C           G   Am
Knowing that love__ is to share.

Bm              C           F#m7        B7
Each one believ - ing that love__ never dies.

F#m7               B7    Em          Am        Am7  D7
Watching her eyes__ and hoping I'm al - ways there.

          G    Am
I will be there

          Bm     C
And ev'rywhere.

G    Am    Bm     C    G
Here, there and ev'rywhere.
```

I'll Have to Say I Love You in a Song

Words and Music by Jim Croce

Melody:

Well, I   know   it's   kind   of   late, __

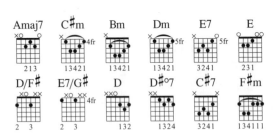

Amaj7   C#m   Bm   Dm   E7   E

D/F#   E7/G#   D   D#°7   C#7   F#m

Intro

‖: Amaj7 | C#m | Bm | Dm   E7 :‖

Verse 1

      Amaj7   **C#m**
Well, I know it's kind of late,

Bm   **E**
  I hope I didn't wake __ ya.

D/F#   E7/G#   Amaj7   **C#m**
  But what I gotta say can't wait.

Bm   **E**   **D/F#   E7/G#**
  I know you'd understand.

Chorus 1

D   **D# 7**
  'Cause ev'ry time I tried to tell you

    C#7   **F#m   D**
The words just came out wrong.

    Amaj7   **E**   **D   Amaj7   E**
So I'll have to say I love __ ya in a song.

Verse 2

     Amaj7   **C♯m**
Yeah, I know it's kind of strange

Bm   **E**
 But ev'ry time I'm near ___ ya,

D/F♯ **E7/G♯** **Amaj7**   **C♯m**
 I just run out of things to say.

Bm   **E** **D/F♯** **E7/G♯**
 I know you'd understand.

Chorus 2   *Repeat Chorus 1*

Guitar Solo ‖: **Amaj7** | **C♯m** | **Bm** | **E** **D/F♯** **E7/G♯** :‖

Chorus 3

    D   **D♯ 7**
 'Cause ev'ry time ____ the time was right

    C♯7   **F♯m** **D**
All the words just came out wrong.

    Amaj7   **E**   **D** **Amaj7** **E**
So I'll have to say I love ___ ya in a song.

Verse 3

    Amaj7   **C♯m**
Yeah, I know it's kind of late,

Bm   **E**
 I hope I didn't wake ___ ya.

D/F♯ **E7/G♯** **Amaj7**   **C♯m**
 But there's somethin' that I just got to say,

Bm   **E** **D/F♯** **E7/G♯**
 I know you'd understand.

Chorus 4   *Repeat Chorus 1*

Outro ‖: **Amaj7** | **C♯m** | **Bm** | **Dm** **E7** :‖
     | **Amaj7**

If You Could Only See

Words and Music by Emerson Hart

If you could on - ly see _____ the _ way _

(Capo 1st fret)

	N.C.		Am		C/G
Chorus 1	If you could only see ___ the way she loves ___ me.				

                                                G5
Then maybe you would un - derstand

G5/F   **G5**   **Am**   **C/G**
Why I feel this way ___ about our love,

                     G5
And what I must do.

G5/F   **G5**   **Am**
If you could on-ly see___ how blue

         C/G   **G5**
Her eyes ___ can be when she says,

G5/F
When she says she loves me.

Interlude 1   ‖: **Asus2**   **Cmaj7/E** | **G6**   **Fmaj7♯11**   :‖

Verse 1   **A5**
Well, you got your reasons

Fmaj7♯11   **Dadd4**
And you got your lies.

A5
And you got your manipulations,

Fmaj7♯11   **Dadd4**
They cut me down to size.

GUITAR CHORD SONGBOOK

Pre-Chorus 1

    Asus2   Cmaj7
Sayin' you love but you ___ don't.

                               G6
You give your love but you ___ won't.

Chorus 2

                    Am   C/G
If you could only see ___ the way she loves ___ me,

                        G5
Then maybe you would un - derstand

G5/F   G5   Am   C/G
Why I feel this way ___ about our love,

                        G5
And what I must do.

G5/F   G5   Am
If you could on-ly see ___ how blue

              C/G   G5
Her eyes ___ can be when she says,

G5/F   G5   Asus2
When she says ___ she loves ___ me.

Interlude 2

Repeat Interlude 1

Verse 2

A5
   Seems the road less traveled

Fmaj7♯11   Dadd4
Shows happiness unrav - eled.

A5
And you got to take a little dirt

                       Fmaj7♯11
To keep what you love.

Dadd4
That's what you gotta do.

Pre-Chorus 2

      Asus2   **Cmaj7**
    Sayin' you love but you ___ don't.

                G6
    You give your love but you ___ won't.

                  Fmaj7♯11   **G6**
    You're stretching out your arms___ to something that's just not there.

    Asus2   **Cmaj7**
    Sayin' you love where you ___ stand.

              G6
    Give your heart when you ___ can.

Chorus 3

                Am   **C/G**
    If you could only see ___ the way she loves ___ me,

              G5
    Then maybe you would un - derstand

    G5/F   **G5**   **Am**   **C/G**
    Why I feel this way ___ about our love,

              G5
    And what I must do.

    G5/F   **G5**   **Am**
    If you could on-ly see ___ how blue

          C/G   **G5**
    Her eyes ___ can be when she says,

    Em
    When she says she loves me.

Guitar Solo   ‖: E   Fmaj7♯11 | G5   Am   :‖ *Play 4 times*

Pre-Chorus 3

Asus2   Cmaj7
   Sayin' you love but you ___ don't.

                        G6
You give your love but you ___ won't.

Fmaj7♯11   G6
   Sayin',

Asus2   Cmaj7
   Sayin' you love where you ___ stand.

                       G6
Give your heart when you ___ can.

Chorus 4

                      Am   C/G
If you could only see___ the way she loves ___ me,

                    G5
Then maybe you would un - derstand

G5/F   G5   Am   C/G
   Why I feel this way ___ about our love,

                 G5
And what I must do.

G5/F   G5   Am
   If you could on-ly see ___ how blue

           C/G   G5
Her eyes ___ can be when she says,

Fmaj7♯11
   When she says she loves me.

Jumper

Words and Music by
Stephan Jenkins

I wish you would step back from _ that ledge, __ my friend.

Fmaj7 C Cadd9 G Am Dadd9 F

Chorus 1

    Fmaj7   **C**   **Cadd9**
I wish you would step back

        G
From that ledge, ___ my friend.

      Fmaj7   **C Cadd9**
You could   cut ties with all the lies

     G
That you've ____ been living in.

   Fmaj7   **C**   **Cadd9**   **G**
And   if you do not want ___ to see me ___ again,

 N.C.   **Fmaj7** **C Cadd9** **G**
I would under-stand,

      Fmaj7 **C Cadd9** **G**
I would under-stand.

Verse 1

Am
The angry boy, a bit too insane,

C
Icing over a secret pain.

G
You know you don't belong.

Am
You're the first to fight, you're way too loud.

C
You're the flash of light on a burial shroud.

G
I know something's wrong.

Am   **Dadd $\frac{4}{9}$**
Well, ev'ryone I know has got a rea - son

C **N.C.**
To say ___ put the past away.

Chorus 2   *Repeat Chorus 1*

Verse 2

Am
Well, he's on the table and he's gone to code

C   **G**
And I do not think anyone knows what they are doing here.

Am
And your friends have left you, you've been dismissed.

C
I never thought it would come to this and I,

G
I want you to know

Am   **Dadd $\frac{4}{9}$**
Ev'ryone's got to face down the de - mons.

C   **N.C.**
Maybe today, ___ you could put the past away.

| Fmaj7   C   Cadd9
| *Chorus 3*   I wish you would step back
| G
| From that ledge, ___ my friend.
| Fmaj7   C Cadd9
| You could   cut ties with all the lies
| G
| That you've ___ been living in.
| Fmaj7   C   Cadd9   G
| And   if you do not want ___ to see me ___ again,
| N.C.   Fmaj7   C Cadd9   G
| I would under-stand,
| Fmaj7   C Cadd9   G
| I would under-stand,
| Fmaj7   C Cadd9   G
| I would under - stand.

Guitar Solo | F   C | G | F   C | G |
                                                            I would understand.
                | F   C | G | F   C | G |
                            I would understand.   Understand.
                | F   C | G | F   C | G |
                | Fmaj7   C | G | Fmaj7   C |
                ‖: G | Fmaj7   C Cadd9 :‖ *Play 4 times*
                | G | Dadd$_9^4$ | C   N.C. |
                                                      Can you put the past away?

Chorus 4

    Fmaj7   **C**   **Cadd9**
    I wish you would step back

              G
From that ledge, ____ my friend.

              Fmaj7
I would understand.

        C   **Cadd9**   **G**
(I wish you would step back ____ from that ledge, ____ my friend.)

            Fmaj7
I would understand.

        C   **Cadd9**   **G**
(I wish you would step back ____ from that ledge, ____ my friend.)

            Fmaj7
And I would under-stand.

        C   **Cadd9**   **G**
(I wish you would step back ____ from that ledge, ____ my friend.)

         Fmaj7
I would under-stand.

        C   **Cadd9**   **G**
(I wish you would step back ____ from that ledge, ____ my friend.)

            Fmaj7   **C Cadd9**   **G**
And I would under - stand.

Outro   ‖:**Fmaj7**   **C** | **G**   :‖ *Play 4 times*

Knockin' on Heaven's Door

Words and Music by Bob Dylan

Melody:

Ma,   take this badge off of me.

Am   G   D/F#   D

231   21 34   1 23   132

Intro

N.C.		Am	
G D/F#		Am	
G D/F#		Am	

Verse 1

G   D/F♯   Am
Ma,   take this badge off of me.

G   D/F♯   Am
I can't use it anymore.

G   D/F♯   Am
It's gettin' dark, too dark to see.

G   D/F♯   Am
I feel like I'm knockin' on heaven's door.

Chorus 1

G   D   Am
Knock, knock, knockin' on heaven's door.

G   D   Am
Knock, knock, knockin' on heaven's door.

G   D   Am
Knock, knock, knockin' on heaven's door.

G   D   Am
Knock, knock, knockin' on heaven's door.

Verse 2

```
G     D/F#      Am
Ma,   take these guns away from me.
G         D/F#              Am
I can't shoot them anymore.
G              D/F#          Am
There's a long, ___ black cloud followin' me.
G              D/F#                Am
Feel like I'm knockin' on heaven's door.
```

Knock, knock, knock.

Chorus 2

```
G              D                Am
Knock, knock, knockin' on heaven's door.
G              D                Am
Knock, knock, knockin' on heaven's door.
```

Guitar Solo

```
‖: G   D/F#  | Am          |          :‖  Play 6 times
```

Verse 3

```
G     D/F#                Am
Ma,   take this badge off of me.
G         D/F#         Am
I can't use it anymore.
G              D/F#           Am
It's gettin' dark, too dark to see.
G              D/F#              Am
I feel like I'm knockin' on heaven's door.
```

Chorus 3

Repeat Chorus 1

Outro

```
‖: G   D/F#   | Am       :‖  Play 4 times
   Oh, oh, oh, oh.
| G
```

Layla

Words and Music by
Eric Clapton and Jim Gordon

Melody:

What _ will you do when you get lone - ly? _____

D5 C5 Bb5 A5 C#m7 G#7 C

D E E7 F#m B A Dm

Intro

‖: D5   C5   Bb5 | C5   D5   :‖ *Play 5 times*

| C5   Bb5 | C5   A5   C5 |

Verse 1

C#m7   G#7
What will you do when you get lone - ly?

C#m7   C   D   E   E7
No one waiting by your ___ side.

F#m   B   E   A
You've been runnin', hidin' much too long.

F#m   B   E
You know it's just your foolish pride.

Chorus 1

A   D5   C5   Bb5
Layla,

C5   D5
Got me on my knees.

C5   Bb5
Layla,

C5   D5
Beggin' dar-lin', please.

C5   Bb5
Layla,

C5   D5   C5   Bb5   C5   A5   C5
Darlin', won't you ease my worried mind?

Verse 2

C#m7   G#7
Tried to give you conso-lation,

C#m7   C   D   E   E7
Your old man had let you down.

F#m   B   E   A
Like a fool, I fell in love with you.

F#m   B   E
You turned my whole world upside down.

Chorus 2

A   D5   C5 B♭5
Layla,

C5   D5
Got me on my knees.

          C5 B♭5
Layla,

C5   D5
Beggin' dar-lin', please.

        C5 B♭5
Layla,

C5   D5   C5 B♭5   C5   A5 C5
Darlin', won't you ease my worried mind?

Verse 3

C#m7   G#7
Make the best of the situ-ation,

C#m7 C D E E7
Before I fin'ly go in-sane.

F#m   B   E   A
Please don't say we'll never find a way.

F#m   B   E
 Tell me all my love's in vain.

Chorus 3

A D5 C5 B♭5
Layla,

C5   D5
Got me on my knees.

    C5 B♭5
Layla,

C5   D5
Beggin' dar-lin', please.

    C5 B♭5
Layla,

C5   D5   C5 B♭5   C5   D5
Darlin', won't you ease my worried mind?

Chorus 4

D5   C5 B♭5
Layla,

C5   D5
Got me on my knees.

        C5 B♭5
Layla,

C5   D5
Beggin' dar-lin', please.

        C5 B♭5
Layla,

C5   D5   C5 B♭5   C5   D5
Darlin', won't you ease my worried mind?

Guitar Solo   ‖: D5 C5   B♭5 | C5   D5   :‖ *Play 8 times*

Chorus 5   *Repeat Chorus 4*

Chorus 6

D5   C5 B♭5
Layla,

C5   D5
Got me on my knees.

        C5 B♭5
Layla,

C5   D5
Beggin' dar-lin', please.

        C5 B♭5
Layla,

C   Dm
Darlin', won't you ease my worried mind?

Learning to Fly

Words and Music by
Jeff Lynne and Tom Petty

Intro ‖: F C | Am Gsus4 :‖ *Play 4 times*

                     F   C   Am   Gsus4
Verse 1   Well, I started out

                     F   C   Am   Gsus4
            Down a dirty road,

            F   C   Am   Gsus4
            Started out

            F   C   Am   Gsus4
            All a-lone.

                     F   C   Am   Gsus4
Verse 2   And the sun went down

                     F   C   Am   Gsus4
            As I crossed the hill

                     F   C   Am   Gsus4
            And the town lit up,

                  F   C   Am   Gsus4
            The world got still.

Chorus 1
       F   C   Am   G
I'm learning to fly,

       F   C   Am   G
But I ain't got wings.

F   C   Am   G
Comin' down

       F   C   Am   G
Is the hardest thing.

Verse 3
       F   C   Am   Gsus4
Well, the good old days

       F   C   Am   Gsus4
May not re-turn,

       F   C   Am   Gsus4
And the rocks might melt,

       F   C   Am   Gsus4
And the sea may burn.

Chorus 2 **Repeat Chorus 1**

Solo ‖: F   C | Am   G   :‖ *Play 4 times*

Verse 4
       F   C   Am   Gsus4
Well, some say life

       F   C   Am   Gsus4
Will beat you down,

       F   C   Am   Gsus4
An' break your heart,

       F   C   Am   Gsus4
And steal your crown.

Verse 5
F   C   Am   Gsus4
So I started out

       F   C   Am   Gsus4
For God knows where,

```
               F      C      Am    Gsus4
          I guess I'll know

               F      C      Am    Gsus4
          When I get there.
```

Chorus 3
```
               F         C    Am   G
          I'm learning to fly

               F         C         Am   G
          A-round the clouds.

          F         C    Am    G
          What goes up

          F         C    Am    G
          Must come down.
```

Interlude   ‖: F   C | Am   G   :‖

Chorus 4
```
               F         C
          ‖: I'm learning to fly,

          Am        G
          (Learning to fly.)

               F    C    Am   G
          But I ain't got wings.

          F    C    Am   G
          Coming down

               F    C    Am   G
          Is the hardest thing.

               F         C
          I'm learning to fly

          Am        G
          (Learning to fly.)

               F    C    Am   G
          A-round the clouds.

               F    C    Am   G
          An' what goes up

          F         C    Am   G
          Must come down.                :‖    *Repeat and fade*
```

Maggie May

Words and Music by
Rod Stewart and Martin Quittenton

Melody:

Wake   up,   Mag - gie,   I _____

Dsus2   G   D   Bm   A   Em   F#m7   Dadd9/F#   Dsus4

Intro

| Dsus2 | G | | | D | G | |
| Dsus2 | G | | | D | Bm G |

Verse 1

      A   **G**   **D**
Wake up, Maggie, I think I got somethin' to say to you.

      A   **G**   **D**
It's late September and I really should be back ___ at school.

  G   **D**
I know I keep you amused,

     G   **A**
But I feel I'm being used.

    Em   **F#m7** **Em**
Oh Maggie, I couldn't have tried any-more.

Chorus 1

Dadd9/F# **Em**   **A**
  You   led me away from home

     Em   **A**
Just to save you from being a-lone.

    Em   **A**   **D**
You stole my heart, and that's ___ what really hurts.

ACOUSTIC ROCK

Verse 2

      A   **G**   **D**
The mornin' sun, when it's in your face, really shows your age.

      A   **G**   **D**
But that don't worry me none; ____ in my eyes you're ev - 'rything.

  G   **D**
I laughed at all of your jokes.

       G   **A**
My love ____ you didn't need to coax.

   Em   **F#m7**   **Em**   **Dadd9/F#**
Oh Maggie, I couldn't have tried any-more.

Chorus 2

   Em   **A**
You led me away from home

     Em   **A**
Just to save you from being a-lone.

   Em   **A**   **D**
You stole my soul, and that's a pain I can do without.

Verse 3

A   **G**   **D**
All I needed was a friend to lend a guiding hand.

      A   **G**
But you turned into a lover, and mother what a lover;

      D
You wore ____ me out.

  G   **D**
All ____ you did was wreck my bed,

     G   **A**
And in the mornin' kick me in the head.

   Em   **F#m7**   **Em**   **Dadd9/F#**
Oh Maggie, I couldn't have tried any-more.

Chorus 3

   Em   **A**
You led me away from home

     Em   **A**
'Cause you didn't wanna be a-lone.

   Em   **A**   **D**
You stole my heart; I couldn't leave you if I tried.

Guitar Solo 1

| Em | A | D | G | |
| Em D | G | D | | |

Verse 4

```
  A              G                   D
I suppose I could col-lect my books and get on back to school.
  A              G                        D
Or steal my daddy's cue ___ and make a living out of playing pool,
  G                  D
Or find myself a rock and roll band
   G               A
That needs a helping hand.
       Em              F#m7        Em        Dadd9/F#
Oh Maggie, I wished I'd never seen your face.
```

Chorus 4

```
            Em            A
You made a first class fool out of me,
            Em            A
But I was blind as a fool can be.
        Em              A           D
You stole my heart, but I love you anyway.
```

Guitar Solo 2

Em	A	D		G	
Em D	G	D			
Em	A	D		G	
Em	G	

Mandolin Solo ‖: D | Dsus4 | G | D :‖ *Play 5 times*

Outro

```
D    Dsus4      G              D
Maggie, I wished I'd nev - er seen your face.
   |          | Dsus4  | G     | D      |
                    Dsus4  G         D
I'll get on back home       one of these days.
‖: D      | Dsus4 | G      | D      :‖ Repeat and fade
```

Like a Rolling Stone

Words and Music by Bob Dylan

Melody:

Once up - on ___ a time you dressed so   fine, _

C	Fmaj7/C	Dm	Em	F	G
32 1	3421	231	23	134211	32 4

Intro
‖: C   Fmaj7/C | C   Fmaj7/C   :‖

Verse 1

C   Dm
Once upon a time you dressed so fine,

Em   F   G
Threw the bums a dime in your prime,   didn't you?

C   Dm   Em
    People call, say, ___ "Beware, doll, you're bound to fall."

             F   G
You thought they were all   a kiddin' you.

F   G
    You used to   laugh about

F   G
    Ev'rybody that was   hangin' out.

F   Em Dm   C
    But now you don't ___ talk so loud.

F   Em Dm   C
    Now you don't seem so proud

Dm   F   G
A-bout havin' to be scrounging   for your next meal.

Chorus 1

                    C   F   G
How does it feel?

                    C   F   G
How does it feel

                        C   F   G
To be without a home,

                        C   F   G
Like a complete un-known,

                        C   F   G
Like a rolling stone?

| C   F | G | |

Verse 2

                C   Dm   Em
Oh, you've   gone to the finest school, al-right, Miss Lonely,

            F   G
But you know you only used to get   juiced in it.

        C   Dm   Em
No-body's ever taught you how to live out on the street

                    F   G
And now you're gonna have to get   used to it.

F   G   F
    You say you never compromise   with the mystery tramp,

                    G   F   Em   Dm   C
But now you   realize   he's not selling any   alibis

        F   Em   Dm   C
As you stare into the vacuum of his eyes

        Dm   F   G
And say, "Do you want to   make a deal?"

```
                       C   F   G
Chorus 2     How does it feel?

                       C   F   G
             How does it feel

                         C   F   G
             To be on your own,

                            C    F    G
             With no direction home,

                           C   F    G
             A complete unknown,

                          C   F    G
             Like a rolling stone?
             | C    F   | G        |          |


                       C                Dm
Verse 3      Oh, you     never turned a-round to see the frowns

             Em                F                    G
                On the jugglers and the clowns when they all did     tricks for you.

             C                   Dm
             Never understood that it ain't no good,

                 Em              F              G
             You shouldn't let other people get your     kicks for you.

             F                                         G
                You used to ride on a chrome horse with your     diplomat

             F                           G
                Who carried on his shoulder a     Siamese cat.

             F          Em            Dm     C
                Ain't it hard ____ when you dis-cover that

             F          Em   Dm        C
                He really wasn't where it's at

             Dm                            F      G
             After he took from you ev'rything     he could steal?
```

Chorus 3

<pre>
              C   F   G
How does it feel?

              C   F   G
How does it feel

              C   F   G
To be on your own,

                  C   F   G
With no direction home,

                   C   F   G
Like a complete unknown,

              C   F   G
Like a rolling stone?
| C   F | G | |
</pre>

Verse 4

<pre>
    C   Dm   Em
    Princess on the steeple and all the pretty people,

              F   G
They're all drinkin', thinkin' that they   got it made.

    C   Dm
    Exchanging all precious gifts,

Em   F   G
    But you better take your diamond ring,

You'd better pawn it, babe.

F   G
    You used to be   so amused

F   G
    At Napoleon in rags   and the language that he used.

F   Em   Dm   C
    Go to him now, he calls you, you can't ___ refuse.

F   Em   Dm   C
    When you ain't got nothin', ___ you got   nothin' to lose.

Dm   F   G
    You're invisible now, you got no secrets   to con-ceal.
</pre>

Chorus 4   *Repeat Chorus 3*

Outro   ‖: C   F | G   :‖ *Repeat and fade*

Lover, You Should've Come Over

Words and Music by Jeff Buckley

Melody:

Look-ing   out   the   door,   I   see   the   rain

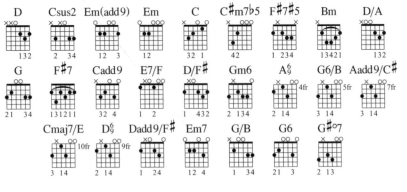

Intro | D | Csus2 | Em(add9) | Em |

Verse 1

D
Looking out the door, I see the rain

    Csus2 Em(add9) Em
Fall upon the fun'ral _____ mourners.

D   C
Pa-rading in a wake of sad re-lations

         Em(add9) Em
As their shoes fill up with water.

Pre-Chorus 1

 C#m7♭5   F#7#5
 Maybe I'm too young

 Bm   D/A G
To keep good love from goin' wrong.

   D   Csus2
But to-night you're on my mind,

 Em(add9)   Em
So ____ you'll never know.

Verse 2

    D
Broken down and hungry for your love,

    Csus2 Em(add9) Em
With no way to ___ feed it.

    D   **C**
Where ___ are you to-night?

        Em(add9) Em
Child, you know how much I need it.

Pre-Chorus 2

  C♯m7♭5   **F♯7♯5**
Too young to hold on,

  Bm   **D/A**   **G** **F♯7**
And too old to just break free and run.

Chorus

  Bm   **Em(add9)**
Well, sometimes a man gets carried away

  Bm   **Em(add9)**
When he feels like he should be havin' his fun,

    Bm   **Em(add9)**
And much too blind to see the damage he's done.

    Cadd9   **C**
And sometimes a man must awake

                  Em   **E7/F**
To find that, really, he has   no one.

D/F♯   **Gm6**
So I'll wait for you,   and I'll burn.

A$^6_9$ **G6/B**
Will I ever see your ___ sweet return?

Aadd9/C♯
Oh, will I ever learn?

Cmaj7/E **D$^6_9$** **Aadd9/C♯** **G6/B**
Oh, _____ lover

   A$^6_9$ **Dadd9/F♯** **D/F♯** **Em**   **Em(add9)**
You ___ should've come   o - ver

             D
'Cause it's not too late.

Csus2 Em(add9) Em Em7 G/B
Mm.

Verse 3

D
Lonely is the room, the bed is made,

          Csus2 Em(add9) Em
The open window lets the ____ rain in.

    D
Burn - ing in the corner is the

C   **Em(add9)**   **Em**
Only one who dreams he had you ____ with him.

Pre-Chorus 3

C♯m7♭5   **F♯7♯5**
  My body turns ____ and yearns

  Bm   **D/A**   **G6**
For a, a sleep that won't ever come.

Verse 4

G♯°7   **D/A**
It's never o - ver,

              Csus2 Em(add9)   **Em**   **Em7**
My kingdom for a kiss up-on her ____ shoulder.

     D/A
Oh, it's never o - ver, all my riches for her smiles

      Csus2 Em(add9) Em
When I slept so soft a - gainst her.

     D/A
It's never o - ver,

           Csus2 Em(add9) Em
All my blood for the sweetness of her ____ laughter.

     D/A
It's never o - ver,

           Csus2 Em(add9) Em
She's a tear that hangs inside my soul for - ever.

C♯m7♭5   **F♯7♯5**
  Ah, but maybe I'm just too young

    Bm   **D/A**   **G**   **Gm6**
To keep ____ good love from ____ goin' wrong.

Outro-Chorus

D/F♯   Gm6
Oh,   oh,

A⁶₉   G6/B   Aadd9/C♯   Cmaj7/E D⁶₉
Oh,   oh, _____ oh.

Aadd9/C♯   G6/B A⁶₉   Dadd9/F♯ D/F♯ Em   Em(add9)
Lover,   you should have come   o - ver.

Yeah, yeah. Well yes, I,

D/F♯   Gm6
I feel too young to hold on,

     A⁶₉   G6/B
And I'm much too old to break free and run.

    Aadd9/C♯   Cmaj7/E
Too deaf, dumb, and blind to see the damage I've ___ done.

D⁶₉   Aadd9/C♯ G6/B   A⁶₉
Sweet lover, _____ you,

          Dadd9/F♯ D/F♯ Em Em(add9)
You should've come   o - ver.

Oh love, well, I'm waiting for you.

D/F♯   Gm6
Lover, lov - er, love,

    A⁶₉
Lover, ___ love, love, love, love,

G6/B   Aadd9/C♯ Cmaj7/E D⁶₉ Aadd9/C♯   G6/B
Love, love, lov - er, lov   -   er,

   A⁶₉   Dadd9/F♯ D/F# Em Em(add9)
You ___ should've come   o - ver

          D   Csus2 Em(add9)
'Cause it's not too late.

The Magic Bus

Words and Music by Peter Townshend

Melody:

Ev - 'ry day __ I   get in the queue __

Tune down 1/2 step:
(low to high) Eb–Ab–Db–Gb–Bb–Eb

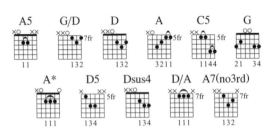

A5   G/D   D   A   C5   G

A*   D5   Dsus4   D/A   A7(no3rd)

Intro

N.C.			A5		
	G/D D	A	C5 G/D
A	C5 G/D	A	G/D D
A G	D	A	C5 G/D

Verse 1

  A   C5 G/D   D
Ev'ry day I get in the queue

  A*   G   D
(Too much, the magic bus.)

    A   C5   G/D   D
To get on the bus that takes ___ me ___ to you.

  A*   G   D
(Too much, the magic bus.)

  A   G/D   D   A*
I'm so nervous, I ___ just sit and smile.

              G   D
(Too much, the magic bus.)

         A   G/D   D
Your house ___ is only an-other mile.

  A*   G   D
(Too much, the magic bus.)

Verse 2

```
A                       C5    G/D  D
Thank you, driver, for getting me  here.
A*          G       D
(Too much, the magic bus.)
        A                   C5    G/D  D
You'll be an inspector, have ___ no___ fear.
A*          G       D
(Too much, the magic bus.)
A                   G/D   D
I don't wanna cause ___ no fuss,
A*          G       D
(Too much, the magic bus.)
      A           G/D  D
But can I buy your magic bus?
A*          G       D
(Too much, the magic bus.)
```

Interlude

```
| A5      |         | N.C   |         |         |
| A5      |         |       |         | D5      |
| A       |         | A*    | C5  G/D |
```

Verse 3

     A   G/D   D

I don't care how much ___ I pay.

     A   C5   G/D

     (Ride the magic bus.)

              A   Dsus4   D

I wanna drive my bus to my baby each day.

     A*   G   D

     (Ride the magic bus.)

   | A |C5 G/D |A |C5 G/D |

   A   N.C.

     I want it, I want it, I want it, I want it, you can't have it.

     A5

I want ___ it.

N.C.   A5

Thruppence and sixpence every day.

N.C.   A5

Just to drive to my baby.

N.C.   A D/A   A7(no3rd)

Lover drives six miles each day.

            D/A   A   D/A   A7(no3rd) D/A A D/A G/D

'Cause I   drive my ba-by ever-y way.

Outro

     A   C5   G/D

     Oh, magic bus.

       A   G/D D

‖: (Magic bus.)   :‖ *Play 10 times*

‖: A |G/D D :‖ *Repeat and fade (w/voc. ad lib.)*

The Man Who Sold the World

Words and Music by David Bowie

Melody:

We passed up - on the stairs, __

Tune down 1/2 step:
(low to high) Eb–Ab–Db–Gb–Bb–Eb

F   Dm   A   C   Db

134211   231   123   32 1   1333   4fr

Intro

| N.C. | | | | |
| F | | Dm | | |

Verse 1

                A
We passed upon the stairs,

                   Dm
We spoke in walls and web.

             A
Although I wasn't there,

             F
He said I was his friend,

              C
Which came as a surprise.

          A
I spoke into his eyes.

           Dm
I thought you died a long,

          C
A long, long time ago.

Chorus 1

        C   **F**
Oh no, __ not me,

     Db   **F**
We never lost control.

          C   **F**
The face ____ to face

     Db
Of a man who sold the world.

Interlude 1

| **A** | | **Dm** | | |
| **F** | | **Dm** | **N.C.** | |

Verse 2

                     A
I laughed and shook his hand

                     Dm
And made my way back home.

               A
I searched afar the land,

                   F
For years and years I roamed.

            C
I gazed a gazy stare.

               A
We walked a million hills.

              Dm
I must have died a long,

               C
A long, long time ago.

Chorus 2	C F Who knows? Not me.

Chorus 2

            C   F
Who knows?   Not me.

    D♭   F
I never lost control.

            C   F
You're face ____ to face

            D♭
With the man who sold the world.

| A | | Dm | | |

Chorus 3

            C   F
Who knows? ____ Not me.

    D♭   F
We never lost control.

            C   F
You're face ____ to face

            D♭
With the man who sold the world.

Interlude 2

| A | | Dm | | |
| F | | | | |

Guitar Solo

Dm		A		
Dm		F		
Dm		A		
Dm		F		
Dm		A		
Dm		F		

Me and Julio Down by the School Yard

Words and Music by Paul Simon

The ma-ma pa-ja - ma rolled___ out of bed,

A   D   E   B   G   D/F#

Intro   ‖: A   D   A | E   :‖ *Play 7 times*

Verse 1

                A
The mama pajama rolled out of bed,

                          D
And she ran to the police station.

                 E
When the papa found out, he began to shout,

                       A   **N.C.**
And he started the investi-gation.

                 E   **A**
It's against the law, it was against the law.

                 E   **A**
What the mama saw, it was against the law.

Verse 2

      A
The mama looked down and spit on the ground

          D
Ev'ry time my name gets mentioned.

      E
The papa said, "Oy, if I get that boy

              A   **N.C.**
I'm gonna stick him in the house of de-tention."

Chorus 1

        D
Well, I'm on my way,

      A
I don't know where I'm goin'.

      D
I'm on my way,

      A   **B**   **E**
I'm takin' my time but I don't know where.

      D   **G**   **A**
Goodbye to Rosie, the Queen of Co-rona.

      G **D/F♯**   **E**   **A**   **D**   **A**   **E**
See you, me and Julio down by the school yard.

      A   **G** **D/F♯**   **E**   **A**   **D**   **A**   **E**
See you, me and Julio down by the school yard.

Interlude

D			A			
D			A	B	E	
D			G	A		
	G	D/F♯ E	A	D A	E	
A	G	D/F♯ E	A	D A	E	
	N.C.					

Verse 3　　　　　　　　　　　　**A**
　　　　　　　　　　Whoa, in a couple of days

　　　　　　　　　　They come and take me away,
　　　　　　　　　　　　　　　　　　　　　D
　　　　　　　　　　But the press let the story leak,
　　　　　　　　　　　　　　　E
　　　　　　　　　　And when the radical priest

　　　　　　　　　　Come to get me released,
　　　　　　　　　　　　　　　　　　A
　　　　　　　　　　We's all on the cover of Newsweek.

　　　　　　　　　　　　　　D
Chorus 2　　　　　　　And I'm on my way,
　　　　　　　　　　　　A
　　　　　　　　　　I don't know where I'm goin'.
　　　　　　　　　　　　D
　　　　　　　　　　I'm on my way,
　　　　　　　　　　　　A　　　**B**　　　**E**
　　　　　　　　　　I'm takin' my time but I don't know where.
　　　　　　　　　　　　D　　　**G**　　　**A**
　　　　　　　　　　Goodbye to Rosie, the Queen of Co-rona.
　　　　　　　　　　　　　　G　**D/F♯**　　**E**　　**A**　　**D**　　**A**　　**E**
　　　　　　　　　　See you, me and Julio down by the school yard.
　　　　　　　　　　　　　A　**G**　**D/F♯**　　**E**　　**A**　　**D**　　**A**　　**E**
　　　　　　　　　　 See you, me and Julio down by the school yard.
　　　　　　　　　　　　　A　**G**　**D/F♯**　　**E**　　**A**　　**D**　　**A**　　**E**
　　　　　　　　　　See you, me and Julio down by the school yard.

Outro　　　　　‖:**A**　　**D**　　**A** |　　**E**　　　　:‖　*Repeat and fade*

More Than Words

Words and Music by
Nuno Bettencourt and Gary Cherone

Intro   ‖: G G/B Cadd9 | Am7 | C | D Dsus4 G   :‖

Verse 1

        G G/B   Cadd9
            Sayin', "I love you"

Am7   C   D   Dsus4 G
Is not the words I want to hear from   you.

G/B   Cadd9   Am7
It's not that I want you   not to say,

    C   D   Dsus4 Em   Am7 D7
But if you on - ly   knew how easy it would be,

    G   D/F#   Em
To show me how you feel.

Chorus 1

          Am7   D7   G7 G7/B C
More than words is all you have to do to make it real.

          Cm   G   Em
Then you wouldn't have to say that you love me,

      Am7   D7   G
'Cause I'd al - ready know.

            D/F#   Em   Bm   C
What would you do__ if my heart was torn in two?

             G/B Am7
More than words to show you feel

```
                D7              G
That your love for me is real.

                    D/F#   Em        Bm     C
What would you say___ if I  took those words a-way?

                    G/B    Am7
Then you couldn't make things new

                D7                  G
Just by say - in', "I love you."
```

Interlude
```
            G  G/B Cadd9                 Am7
                    La, dee, da , la, dee, da,

                    C
Dee, dai, dai, da.

D     Dsus4 G      G/B  Cadd9
More than   words.

                        Am7    D7
La, dee, da, dai, da.
```

Verse 2
```
            G  G/B         Cadd9    Am7
                    Now that I've tried to     talk to you

        C       D   Dsus4  G
And make you un - der  -   stand,

G/B      Cadd9           Am7
    All you___ have to do is close your eyes

        C         D   Dsus4  Em
And just reach out your   hands

        Am7            D7              G    D/F#  Em
And___ touch me, hold me close, don't ever let me go.
```

Chorus 2
```
                Am7    D7      G7        G7/B  C
            More than words is all I ever needed you___ to show.

                Cm          G
Then you wouldn't have to say

                Em
That you love me,
```

```
                Am7   D   D7b9/A    G
'Cause I'd al - read - y         know.

                            D/F#
What would you do

            Em      Bm    C
If my heart was torn in two?

                            G/B  Am7
More than words to show you  feel

            D7              G
That your love for me is real.

                            D/F#
What would you say

            Em        Bm      C
If I took those words a-way?

                            G/B   Am7
Then you couldn't make things new

                D7          G        G/B  Cadd9
Just by say - ing "I love    you."
```

```
                        Am7
Outro       ‖: La, dee, da, dai, dai,

                    C
Dee, dai, dai, da.

D    Dsus4  G    G/B  Cadd9
More than   words.       :‖  Play 3 times

                        Am7
La, dee, da, dai, dai,

                    C
Dee, dai, dai, da.

D    Dsus4  G          D/F#
More than   words.

Dm(add9)/F    Esus4
Oo, oo, oo, oo,

                Am7      D
Oo, oo,        oo.

N.C.      G      Csus2  G/B  Gm/Bb  Am7  G
More than words.
```

Mother Nature's Son

Words and Music by
John Lennon and Paul McCartney

Melody:

Born _ a   poor _ young   coun - try _ boy,

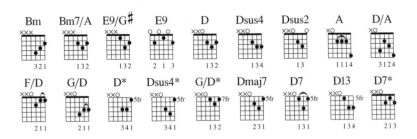

Intro

Bm Bm7/A	E9/G# E9
D Dsus4	Dsus2 Dsus4 D
Dsus2 D Dsus4 D	Dsus2 D Dsus2 D

Verse 1

  D   Dsus4   D
Born a poor young country boy,

  Bm   Bm7/A E9/G#   E9
Mother Nature's son.

  A D/A   A D/A A
All day long___ I'm sitting

     D/A   A   D/A
Sing - ing songs___ for ev - 'ryone.

| D   F/D | G/D   D |
| F/D | G/D   D |

Verse 2

```
D      Dsus4        D
```
Sit be-side a mountain stream,

```
Bm     Bm7/A E9/G♯  E9
```
See her waters rise.

```
A  D/A   A D/A A
```
Lis-ten to__ the pretty

```
   D/A     A   D/A      D   F/D   G/D   D
```
Sound__ of mu - sic as she flies.

Bridge 1

```
Dsus4 D*    Dsus4* D* G/D*        D*
```
Do, doot, do, do, do,   do, do, doodle, do.

```
    Dsus4* D* G/D*      D*   Dmaj7   D7
```
Do, do, do,   do, do, doodle, do.

```
   D13  D7      G/D   Gm/D    D
```
Mm, do, ___ do.

Verse 3

```
D      Dsus4        D
```
Find me in my field of grass,

```
Bm     Bm7/A  E9/G♯ E9
```
Mother Nature's son.

```
A    D/A      A D
```
Sway-ing dais - ies

```
A     D/A  A        D/A     D   F/D   G/D   D
```
Sing a la - zy song beneath__ the sun.

Bridge 2

      Dsus4 D*   Dsus4* D* G/D*   D*
Do, doot, do, do, do,   do, doodle, doodle, do.

          Dsus4* D* G/D*   D*   Dmaj7 D7
Do, do, do,   do, do, doodle, do.

          D13 D7   G/D Gm/D
Mm, do, do, do, do, do,

          D   Dsus4
Yeah, yeah, yeah.

Verse 4

D   Dsus4   D
Mm, mm, mm, mm, mm,

Bm Bm7/A   E9/G♯ E9
Oo, oo.

A D/A A D/A   A   D/A A   D/A   D F/D G/D D
Mm, _____ mm, _____ mm, __ do-wah.

      F/D
Oo, ah,

G/D   D7*
Mother Nature's son.

Mrs. Robinson

Words and Music by Paul Simon

Melody:

And here's to you, ___

(Capo 2nd fret)

E   A7   D   G   C   C/B   Am   D7   Em

Intro

‖: **E** | | | :‖

E
De, de, de, de, de, de, de, de, de, de, de, de, de.

A7
Do, do, do, do, do, do, do, do, do.

D   **G**   **C**   **C/B**   **Am**
  De, de, de, de, de, de, de, de, de, de, de, de, de.

|**E** | |**D7** | |

Chorus 1

          G   **Em**
And here's to you, ___ Mrs. Rob - inson,

G   **Em**   **C**
Jesus loves you more ___ than you will know.

            D
Whoa, whoa, whoa.

          G   **Em**
God bless you, please, Mrs. Rob - inson,

G   **Em**   **C**
Heaven holds a place ___ for those who pray.

        Am   **E**
Hey, hey, hey, ___ hey, hey, hey.

Verse 1

    E
We'd like to know a little bit about you for our files.

    A7
We'd like to help you learn to help yourself.

D7   **G**   **C** **C/B** **Am**
Look around you, all ___ you see are sympa-thetic eyes.

E   **D7**
Stroll around the grounds un-til you feel at home.

Chorus 2   *Repeat Chorus 1*

Verse 2

    E
Hide it in a hiding place where no one ever goes.

A7
Put it in your pantry with your cupcakes.

D   **G**   **C** **C/B**   **Am**
It's a little se - cret, just the Rob - in-son's affair.

E   **D7**
Most of all you've got to hide ___ it from the kids.

Chorus 3

          G   **Em**
Coo, coo, cachoo, ___ Mrs. Rob - inson,

G   **Em**   **C**
Jesus loves you more ___ than you will know.

        D
Whoa, whoa, whoa.

       G   **Em**
God bless you, please, Mrs. Rob - inson,

G   **Em**   **C**
Heaven holds a place ___ for those who pray.

      Am   **E**
Hey, hey, hey, ___ hey, hey, hey.

Verse 3

    E

       Sitting on a sofa on a Sunday afternoon,

    A7

       Going to the candidate's debate.

    D   G

       Laugh about it, shout about it,

    C   C/B   Am

    When you've got to choose.

    E   D7

       Ev'ry way you look at this you lose.

Chorus 4

                                G   Em

    Where have you gone, ___ Joe DiMag - gio?

    G   Em   C

    A nation turns its lonely eyes to you.

                  D

    Woo, woo, woo.

                  G   Em

    What's that you say, Mrs. Rob - inson,

    G   Em   C

    "Joltin' Joe" has left and gone away.

               Am   E

    Hey, hey, hey, ___ hey, hey, hey.

Intro

    ‖: E | :‖ *Repeat and fade*

My Sweet Lord

Words and Music by George Harrison

Melody:

My __ sweet Lord, __

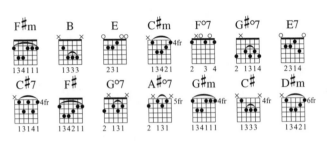

F#m   B   E   C#m   F°7   G#°7   E7
C#7   F#   G°7   A#°7   G#m   C#   D#m

Intro

```
|: F#m      B  |          :|  Play 4 times
|  E       C#m |       E |
|          C#m |       E |
|          F°7 |  G#°7    |
|  F#m      B  |          |
```

Verse 1

                F#m   B
My sweet Lord,

            F#m   B
Mmm, my Lord.

B   F#m   B
   Mmm, my Lord.

Chorus 1

               E   C#m
I really want to see You.

              E   C#m
Really want to be with You.

           E
Really want to see You, Lord,

       F°7   G#°7   F#m   B
But it takes so long, my Lord.

Verse 2

Repeat Verse 1

Chorus 2

                  E   C#m
I really want to know You.

                  E   C#m
Really want to go with You.

                  E
Really want to show You, Lord,

         F°7   G#°7   F#m   B
But it won't take long, my Lord.

Verse 3

                  F#m   B
My sweet Lord.

                  F#m   B
Mmm, my Lord.

                  F#m   B
My sweet Lord.

Chorus 3

                  E
Really want to see You.

                  E7
Really want to see You.

Bridge

                  C#7
Really want to see You, Lord.

                  F#
Really want to see You, Lord,

         G°7   A#°7   G#m   C#
But it takes so long, my Lord.

Verse 4

                  G#m   C#
My sweet Lord.

                  G#m   C#
Mmm, my Lord,

                  G#m   C#
My, my, my Lord.

Chorus 4

           F♯   D♯m
I really want to know You.

              F♯   D♯m
Really want to go with You.

            F♯
Really want to show You, Lord,

    G°7   A♯°7   G♯m   C♯
And it won't take long, my ___ Lord.

         G♯m   C♯   G♯m   C♯
Mmm,   my sweet Lord.

         G♯m   C♯
My, my Lord.

Interlude

| F♯ | D♯m | | | F♯ | D♯m | | |
| F♯ | G°7 | | A♯°7 | G♯m | C♯ | | |

                                   Mmm, my Lord.

| G♯m | C♯ | | G♯m | |
           My, my, my Lord.

Verse 5

    C♯   G♯m   C♯
Oh, hmm, my sweet Lord.

        G♯m
Ooh.

Chorus 5

   C♯   F♯   D♯m
   Now I really want to see You.

             F♯   D♯m
I really want to be with you.

           F♯
Really want to see you, Lord,

    G°7   A♯°7   G♯m   C♯
But it takes so long, my___ Lord.

         G♯m   C♯   G♯m   C♯
My Lord,   my, my, my Lord.

          G♯m   C♯   G♯m
My sweet Lord.   My sweet Lord.

Outro

     C♯   G♯m
‖: My ___ Lord. :‖ *Repeat and fade*

Pinball Wizard

Words and Music by Pete Townshend

Melody:

Ev - er since I was a young _ boy,

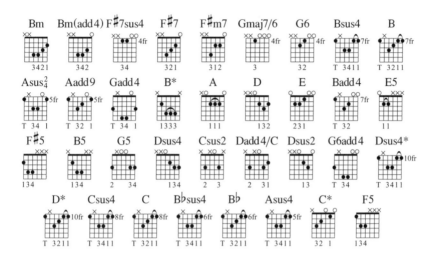

Bm   Bm(add 4)   F#7sus4   F#7   F#m7   Gmaj7/6   G6   Bsus4   B

Asus²₄   Aadd 9   Gadd 4   B*   A   D   E   Badd 4   E5

F#5   B5   G5   Dsus4   Csus2   Dadd4/C   Dsus2   G6add 4   Dsus4*

D*   Csus4   C   Bbsus4   Bb   Asus4   C*   F5

Intro

Bm	Bm(add4)	F#7sus4	F#7	
F#m7	Gmaj7/6	G6	F#7	
	‖: Bsus4	B	:‖	*Play 4 times*

Verse 1

        Bsus4   B
Ever since I was a young boy, I played the silver ball.

        Asus²₄   Aadd9
From Soho down to Brighton, I must've played 'em all.

        Gadd4
But I ain't seen nothin' like him in any amusement hall.

        F#7sus4   N.C.   B*   A   D   E
That deaf, dumb and blind kid sure plays a mean pin-ball.

| B*   A   D | E | |

Verse 2

    Bsus4   **Badd4**

He stands like a statue, becomes part of the machine.

Asus$^2_4$ **Aadd9**

Feelin' all the bumpers, always playing clean.

Gadd4   **G6**

Plays by intuition, the digit counters fall.

    F♯7sus4   **N.C.**   **B* A D E**

That deaf, dumb and blind kid sure plays a mean pin-ball.

| **B***   **A** **D** | **E** |

Chorus 1

    E5   **F♯5** **B5**

He's a pin - ball   wizard.

    E5   **F♯5** **B5**

There has to be a twist.

    E5 **F♯5** **B5**   **G5**   **D**   **Dsus4** **D**

A pin - ball   wizard's got such a supple wrist.

Bridge

D   **Csus2**   **D**   **Dadd4/C**

How do you think he does ____ it? (I don't know.)

Dsus2   **Csus2** **D**

What makes him so good?

Verse 3

Bsus4   Badd4
Ain't got no distractions, can't hear no buzzers and bells.

$Asus^2_4$ Aadd9
Don't see no lights a flashin', plays by sense of smell.

G6add4   G6
Always gets a replay, never seen him fall.

F♯7sus4   N.C.   B* A D E
That deaf, dumb and blind kid sure plays a mean pin-ball.

| B*   A D | E |

Chorus 2

E5   F♯5 B5 E5   F♯5 B5
I thought I   was the Bally table king

E5 F♯5 B5   G5   D Dsus4 D
But I just handed my pinball crown to him.

Interlude   ‖: Dsus4* | D*   :‖ *Play 4 times*

Verse 4

Dsus4*   D*
Even on my fav'rite table, he can beat my best.

Csus4   C
His dis-ciples lead him in and he just does the rest.

B♭sus4   B♭
He's got crazy flipper fingers, never seen him fall.

Asus4   N.C.   D C* F5
That deaf, dumb and blind kid sure plays a mean pin-ball.

Outro   ‖: B♭sus4 | :‖ *Repeat and fade*

Night Moves

Words and Music by Bob Seger

Melody:

I was a lit-tle too tall, could a used a

(Capo 1st fret)

G   F   C   D   Em   Cmaj7   G7   Bm   Am

Intro   ‖: G | F C | | F   :‖

Verse 1

G   F   C
I was a little too tall, could a used a few pounds.

                                                 F
Tight pants, points, hardly renown.

G   F   C
She was a black-haired beauty with big, dark eyes,

                                                 F
And points all her own, sittin' way up high,

| G | F C |

                 F
Way up firm and high.

G   F   C
Out past the cornfields, where the woods got heavy,

                                                 F
Out in the back seat of my sixty Chevy,

G   F   C
Working on myst'ries without any clues.

Chorus 1

    D   **Em**   **D** **C**
Work-in' on our night moves,

    D   **Em**   **D** **C**
Try'n' to make some   front page, drive-in news.

    D   **Em**   **D** **C** **Cmaj7**
Work-in' on our night moves,

G   **F** **C**
In the summertime.

  F **G**   **F** **C**   **F**
Mm,   in the sweet summertime.

Verse 2

G   **F** **C**
We weren't in love. Oh, no, far from it.

                         F
We weren't searchin' for some pie-in-the-sky summit.

G   **F** **C**
We were just young and restless and bored,

              F
Living by the sword.

G   **F** **C**
And we'd steal away ev'ry chance we could,

                   F
To the backroom, to the alley, or the trusty woods.

G   **F** **C**
I used her, she used me, but neither one cared,

We were gettin' our share.

	D Em D C
Chorus 2	Work-in' on our night moves,

D   Em   D C
Tryin' to lose the   awkward teen-age blues.

D   Em   D C Cmaj7
Work-in' on our night moves,   mm,

G   F   C
And it was summertime.

F G   F   C   D
Mm,   sweet summertime, sum-mertime.

Interlude 1 | Em | D |G |G7 |

Bridge
Cmaj7 G
And, oh, the wonder.

Cmaj7
We felt the lightning. Yeah,

F
And we waited on the thunder.

D   G
Waited on the thunder.

Verse 3

G
I awoke last night to the sound of thunder.

Cmaj7
"How far off?" I sat and wondered.

G
Started humming a song from nineteen-sixty-two.

Cmaj7   Em
Ain't it funny how the night moves?

C   Em
When you just don't seem to have as much to lose.

C   Em
Strange how the night moves

C Cmaj7
With autumn closing in.

Interlude 2

| G | | | | F C |
| | | F | G | | F C |
Mm.   Night moves.

| | | F | |
Mm.

Outro

       G   F   C
‖: (Night moves.) Night moves.

                F
(Night moves.) Yeah.   :‖ *Play 7 times*

  G
(Night moves.) Night moves.

F C   D
I remember. Oh!

Em
Ooh, ooh.

Bm
Ah, yeah, yeah, yeah, yeah.

Am   C   G
Ah,   ah.   I remember, I remember.

No Rain

By Blind Melon

Melody:

All   I   can   say ____

E · · D · · A · · G5
231   132   123   2 34

Intro

E				
	D	E	D	E
	D	E	D	

Chorus 1

    E   D
All I can say is that my life is pretty plain.

    A   G5   E
I like watching the puddles gather rain.

                         D
And all I can do is just pour some tea for two

        A   G5   E
And speak my point of view but it's not sane.

It's not sane.

Verse 1

    E   D   E
I just want someone to say to me,

D
"No, oh, oh, oh.

E   D   E   D
I'll always be__ there when you wake."

E   D   E   D
You know I'd like to keep my cheeks dry today.

E   D   E
So stay with me and I'll have it made.

           D
(I'll have it made.)

Chorus 2

      E   D
And I don't understand why I sleep all day

      A   G5   E
And I start to complain__ that there's no rain.

                      D
And all I can do is read a book to stay awake,

      A   G5   E
And it rips my life away__ but it's a great es-cape.

Escape, escape, escape.

Solo   ‖: E   D | :‖ *Play 8 times*

Chorus 3

      E   D
All I can say is that my life is pretty plain.

           A
You don't like my point of view;

G5   E
You think that I'm in-sane.

It's not sane. It's not sane.

Verse 2   *Repeat Verse 1*

Outro   D   E
        ‖: (I'll have it made.) I'll have it made.   :‖ *Play 9 times*

Norwegian Wood
(This Bird Has Flown)

Words and Music by
John Lennon and Paul McCartney

Melody:

I once had a girl, __

(Capo 2nd fret)

D   Cadd9   G/B   Dm   G   Em7   A

Intro ‖: D | | **Cadd9 G/B** D :‖

Verse 1

D
I once had a girl,

Or should I say
Cadd9   G/B D
She once had me?

She showed me her room,

Isn't it good,
Cadd9   G/B D
Norwe - gian wood?

Bridge 1

       Dm   **G**
She asked me to stay and she told me to sit anywhere.
       Dm   **Em7** **A**
So I looked around and I noticed there wasn't a chair.

Verse 2

D
I sat on a rug

Biding my time,

Cadd9　G/B　D
Drinking her　wine.

We talked until two,

And then she said,

Cadd9　G/B　D
"It's time for　bed."

Interlude

‖: D ｜ ｜ Cadd9 G/B｜ D :‖

Bridge 2

Dm
She told me she worked in the morning and started to laugh.   G

Dm
I told her I didn't and crawled off to sleep in the bath.   Em7　A

Verse 3

D
And when I awoke

I was alone,

Cadd9　G/B　D
This bird had　flown.

So I lit a fire,

Isn't it good,

Cadd9　G/B　D
Norwe - gian　wood?

Outro

｜D ｜ ｜ Cadd9 G/B｜ D

Not Fade Away

Words and Music by
Charles Hardin and Norman Petty

| E | A/E | A | D/A |
| 2 3 1 | 1 1 1 | 1 1 1 | 3 1 2 |

Intro

| E A/E E | A/E E | A E | A E |

Verse 1

  E   A   D/A A
I wanna tell ya how it's gonna be.

    E   A E   A E
Uh, you're gonna give your love to me.

                              A   D/A A
I'm gonna love you night and day.

Chorus 1

      E   A E   A E
Oh, love is love, not fade away.

                            A   E
Uh, well, love is love, not fade away.

Verse 2

     E   A   D/A   A
Uh, my love's bigger than a Cadillac.

    E   A E   A E
I ____try to show it and you drive me back.

                          A   D/A   A
Uh, your love for me has got to be real,

E   A E   A E
For you to know just how I feel.

Chorus 2

```
E              A  E        A  E
```
Uh, love real, not fade away.

```
                A  E      A  E
```
Uh, well, love real, not fade away.   Yeah!

Interlude

```
‖:A   D/A  A |    D/A  A │E     A  E |      A  E:‖
|     A  E |
```

Verse 3

```
E                      A    D/A A
```
I'm gonna tell ya how it's gonna be.

```
E                  A  E     A  E
```
Uh, you're gonna give your love to me.

```
                 A      D/A  A
```
A love that lasts more than one day.

Chorus 3

```
           E        A  E   A  E
```
Uh well, love is love, not fade away.

```
                  A  E   A  E
```
Well, love is love, not fade away.

Outro

```
       E    A    E       A    E
```
Well, love is love, not fade away.

```
       A        E     A    E
```
L-love, love, 'll not fade away.

```
         A      E
```
Not fade a-way.

```
         A      E
```
Not fade a-way.   *Fade out*

Only Wanna Be With You

Words and Music by Darius Carlos Rucker, Everett Dean Felber,
Mark William Bryan and James George Sonefeld

(Capo 2nd fret)

E   A6/9   F#7sus4   Asus2   Bsus4

Intro
| E   A6/9 | E   A6/9| E   A6/9 | F#7sus4 |
‖: E   A6/9 :‖ *Play 4 times*

Verse 1

E   A6/9 E   A6/9
You and me, we come from diff'rent worlds,

E   A6/9   E   A6/9
You like to laugh at me when I look__ at other girls.

E   A6/9 E   A6/9
Sometimes you're crazy,   and you wonder why

E   A6/9   E   A6/9
I'm such a baby 'cause the Dol - phins make me cry.

Chorus 1

        F#7sus4
But there's nothin' I can do,

Asus2   E   A6/9   E   A6/9
I've been lookin' for a girl like you.

erse 2

   E   **A6/9**   **E**   **A6/9**
You look at me, you got nothing left to say.

   E   **A6/9**   **E**   **A6/9**
I moan and pout at you un-til I get my___ way.

   E   **A6/9** **E**   **A6/9**
I won't dance,   you won't sing.

   E   **A6/9**
I just want to love you,

        E   **A6/9**
But you want to wear my___ ring.

          F#7sus4

horus 2 But there's nothin' I can do,

Asus2   **E** **A6/9** **E** **A6/9**
   I only want to be with you.

        Asus2
You can call me your fool,

Bsus4   **E** **A6/9** **E** **A6/9**
   I only want to be with you.

   E   **A6/9**   **E**   **A6/9**
erse 3 Put on a little Dylan,   sittin' on a fence.

   E   **A6/9**
I say, "That line is great."

    E   **A6/9**
You ask me what I meant by,

   E   **A6/9**
"Said I shot a man named Gray,

   E   **A6/9**
Took his wife to Italy.

   E   **A6/9**
She inherits a million bucks,

    E   **A6/9**
And when she died it came to me."

Chorus 3

       F#7sus4
I can't help it if I'm lucky,"

Asus2   **E   A6/9   E   A6/9**
   I only want to be with you.

Asus2
   Ain't Bobby so cool?

Bsus4   **E**
   I only want to be with you.

Solo   ‖: **E A6/9** | **E   A6/9** :‖ *Play 8 times*

Chorus 4

        F#7sus4
Yeah, I'm tangled up in blue,

Asus2   **E   A6/9   E   A6/9**
   I only want to be with you.

       F#7sus4
You can call me your fool,

Bsus4   **E   A6/9   E   A6/9**
   I only want to be with you.

|**E A6/9** | **E   A6/9** |

Verse 4

```
      E           A6/9     E              A6/9
      Sometimes I wonder    if we'll ever end.

      E           A6/9
      You get so mad at me

            E             A6/9
      When I go out with my friends.

      E                A6/9
      Sometimes you're crazy,

      E                   A6/9
      And you wonder why.

      E            A6/9
      I'm such a baby, yeah,

            E              A6/9
      The Dol - phins make me cry.
```

Chorus 5

```
            F#7sus4
      But there's nothin' I can do,

      Asus2                  E   A6/9  E   A6/9
          I only want to be with you.

            F#7sus4
      You can call me your fool,

      Asus2                  E   A6/9  E   A6/9
          I only want to be with you.

            Asus2         Bsus4
      Yeah, I'm tangled up in blue,

                  E   A6/9   E
      I only want to be with you.

      A6/9              E   A6/9   E
    ‖: I only want to be with you.        :‖   *Play 4 times*
```

Pink Houses

Words and Music by John Mellencamp

Melody:

Well, there's a black ___ man _

Open G tuning:
(low to high) D–G–D–G–B–D

| G | C | F | D | G* | C* | D* | F6sus2 | F$^6_9$ | Cadd9 |

Intro ‖: G |C   G   :‖ *Play 4 times*

Verse 1

                          G
Well, there's a black ___ man with a black cat,

Livin' in a black neighborhood.

He's got an interstate runnin' through his front yard,
                      F   **C**   **G**
And you know he thinks ___ he's got it so good.

And there's a woman in the kitchen,

Cleaning up the evening slop.
         F
And he looks at her and says,"Hey darlin',
C   **G**
    I can remember when you could stop a clock."

GUITAR CHORD SONGBOOK

Chorus 1

       C   **G**
Oh, but ain't that Amer-ica, for you and me.

       C   **G**
Ain't that Ameri - ca, something to see, ___ baby.

       C   **D**
Ain't that Amer-ica, home of the free, ___ yeah.

        C
Little pink houses for you and me.

G* **C**
Oh, ___ yeah, for you and me.

G **C G** **C G**
 Ow!

Verse 2

         G
Well, there's a young ___ man in a tee-shirt,

List'nin' to a rock 'n' roller station.

He's got a greasy hair and a greasy smile.

      F   **C**   **G**
He says, "Lord, ___ this must be my destina - tion."

'Cause they told me when I was younger,

Sayin', "Boy, you're gonna be president."

      F   **C**
But just like ev'rything else, those old cra - zy dreams

      G
Just kinda came and went.

Chorus 2

              C*   **G**
Oh, but ain't that Amer-ica, for you and me.

         C*   **G**
Ain't that Amer-ica, something to see, ___ baby.

         C*   **D***
Ain't that Amer-ica, home of the free, ___ yeah.

        C*
Little pink houses for you and me.

              G   **C** **G**
Oh, build them, baby, for you and me.

| | **C** **G** | | **C** **G** |

Interlude   ‖: **F6sus2** | **C*** | **G** | :‖ *Play 4 times*
| | |

Verse 3

          G
Well, there's peo - ple, and more people.

What do they know, know, know?

Go to work in some high rise
      F   **C**   **G**
And va-cation down at the Gulf of Mexico, ___ ooh, yeah.

And there's winners and there's losers,

But they ain't no big deal.
        F$_9^6$ **Cadd9**
'Cause the sim - ple man, baby, pays for the thrills,

        G*
The bills, the pills that kill.

Chorus 3

        C*   **G**
Oh, but ain't that Amer-ica, for you and me.

        C*   **G**
Ain't that Amer-ica, something to see, ___ baby.

        C*   **D***
Ain't that Amer-ica, home of the free, ___ yeah.

        C*
Little pink houses for you and me. Ooh.

G
  Ooh, yeah!

Chorus 4

        C*   **G**
Oh, but ain't that Amer-ica, for you and me.

        C*   **G**
Ain't that Amer-ica, something to see, ___ baby.

        C*   **D***
Ain't that Amer-ica, home of the free.

                             C*
Ooh, yeah, yeah, yeah, yeah, yeah, yeah, yeah.

                   G
Little pink houses, babe, for you and me.

Outro

C   **G**
Ooh, yeah.

C   **G**   **C** **G**   **C** **G***
Ooh, yeah.

Quicksand

Words and Music by David Bowie

Melody:

I'm clos-er to the Gold - en Dawn,

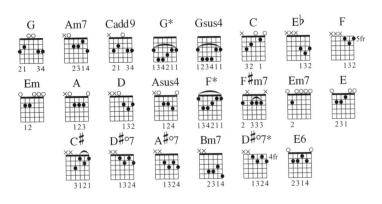

G   Am7   Cadd9   G*   Gsus4   C   E♭   F

Em   A   D   Asus4   F*   F♯m7   Em7   E

C♯   D♯°7   A♯°7   Bm7   D♯°7*   E6

Intro ‖: G   Am7 | | G   Am7 | :‖

Verse 1

Cadd9
I'm closer to the Golden Dawn,

                      G*   **Gsus4 G***
Immersed in Crowley's uniform of ____ imagery.

Cadd9
I'm living in a silent film,

    C   **G**
Por-traying Himmler's sacred realm of dream ____ reality.

    E♭
I'm frightened by the total goal,

F
Drawing to the ragged hole,

    G   **Em**   **C**
And I ain't got the power any-more.

                   G   **Am7**   **A**
No, I ain't got the power any-more.

Verse 2

          D
I'm the twisted name on Garbo's eyes,

                                 A   **Asus4**   **A**
Living proof of Churchill's lies, I'm __ destiny.

          D
I'm torn between the light and dark,

                              A   **Asus4**   **A**
Where others see their target's divine __ symmetry.

F*
Should I kiss the viper's fang

   G*
Or herald loud the death of Man?

   A   **F♯m7**   **Em7** **D**
I'm sinking in the quicksand of my   thoughts,

                       A   **Asus4**   **A**
And I ain't got the power any-more.

Chorus 1

   A   **E**   **C♯** **F♯m7**
Don't believe ____ in your - self,

            D♯°7   **E**
Don't deceive ____ with belief,

           A♯°7   **Bm7**
Knowledge comes ____ with death's release,

   D♯°7* **A**   **F♯m7** **E6** **E**
Ah, _____ ah. _____

A   **E**   **C♯** **F♯m7**
  Don't believe ____ in your - self,

          D♯°7   **E**
Don't deceive ____ with belief,

          A♯°7   **Bm7**
Knowledge comes ____ with death's release,

   D♯°7* **A**   **F♯m7** **E6** **E**
Ah, _____ ah. _____

Verse 3

    D
I'm not a prophet or a Stone Age man,

                                             A
Just a mortal with potential of a superman I'm __ living on.

    D
I'm tethered to the logic of homo sapien,

                                       A
Can't take my eyes from the great salvation of bullshit faith.

    F*
If I don't explain what you ought to know,

      G*
You can tell me all about it, on the next Bardot.

  A   **F♯m7**   **D**
I'm sinking in the quicksand of my   thoughts,

                              A   **Asus4**   **A**   **Asus4**
And I ain't got the power anymore.

Chorus 2

    A   **E**   **C♯** **F♯m7**
Don't believe ____ in your - self,

           D♯°7   **E**
Don't deceive ____ with belief,

           A♯°7   **Bm7**
Knowledge comes ____ with death's release,

    D♯°7* **A**   **F#m7** **E6** **E**
Ah, _____ ah. _____

Outro   *Repeat Chorus 2 till fade*

Road Trippin'

Words and Music by Anthony Kiedis,
Flea, John Frusciante and Chad Smith

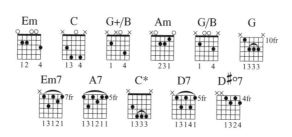

Intro   ‖: Em | | C | G+/B :‖

Verse 1

    Em   C   G+/B
Road trippin' with my two fav'rite al-lies.

    Em   C   G+/B
Fully loaded, we got snacks and supplies.

    Em   C   G+/B
It's time to leave this town, it's time to steal away.

    Em   C   G+/B
Let's go get lost any-where in the U.S.A.

    Em   C   G+/B
Let's go get lost, let's go get lost.

Chorus 1

Em   C   G+/B
Blue, you sit so pretty west of the one.

Em   C
Sparkles light with yellow icing,

   G+/B   Em
Just a mirror for the sun.

C   G+/B   Em
Just a mirror for the sun.

C   G+/B   Am   G/B   C   G
Just a mirror for the sun.

Am   G/B   C   G
These smiling eyes ___ are just a mirror for...

Verse 2

Em   C   G+/B
So much as came before those battles lost and won.

Em   C   G+/B
This life is shining more for-ever in the sun.

Chorus 2

Em   C   G+/B
Now let us check our heads and let us check the surf.

Em   C   G   Em
Staying high and dry's more trouble than it's worth in the sun.

C   G+/B   Em
Just a mirror for the sun.

C   G+/B   Am   G/B   C   G
Just a mirror for the sun. _____

Am   G/B   C   G
These smiling eyes ___ are just a mirror for…

Interlude

‖: Em7 | A7 | C* | D7 |
| Em7 | A7 | C* | D#°7 :‖
| | | | |

Verse 3

    Em   C   G+/B
In Big Sur we take some time to linger on.

    Em   C   G+/B
We three hunky dories got our snake finger on.

    Em   C   G+/B
Now let us drink the stars, it's time to steal away.

    Em   C   G+/B
Let's go get lost right here in the U.S.A.

    Em   C   G+/B
Let's go get lost, let's go get lost.

Chorus 3

    Em   C   G+/B
Blue, you sit so pretty west of the one.

    Em   C
Sparkles light with yellow icing,

    G+/B   Em
Just a mirror for the sun.

C   G+/B   Em
Just a mirror for the sun.

C   G+/B   Am   G/B   C   G
Just a mirror for the sun.

    Am   G/B   C   G
These smiling eyes ___ are just a mirror for…

    Am   G/B   C   G
These smiling eyes ___ are just a mirror for…

    Am   G/B   C   G
Your smiling eyes ___ are just a mirror for…

Outro

‖: Em | | | :‖ *Play 3 times*

Run Around

Words and Music by John Popper

G   C   Am   D

32 4   32 1   231   132

Intro   ‖: G   C   Am| D   :‖   *Play 6 times*

Verse 1

        G   C Am   D
Oh, once up-on a midnight dearie

       G   C   Am   D
I woke   with some-thing in my head.

   G   C   Am   D
I couldn't es-cape the memo-ry

        G   C   Am   D
Of a phone__ call and of__ what you said.

        G   C   Am   D
Like a game show contestant with a parting gift,

        G C   Am   D
I could not   be-lieve my eyes

        G   C   Am   D
When I saw   through the voice of a trusted friend

          G   C   Am   D
Who needs to humor me and tell me lies.

        G   C   Am   D
Yeah, hu - mor me and tell me lies.

        G   C   Am   D
And I'll lie   too, and say I don't mind,

```
         G       C   Am      D
And as we seek,__ so shall we find.

         G            C         Am    D
And when you're feel-ing open I'll still be here,

      G        C            Am    D
But not without a certain de-gree of fear

      G      C  Am           D
Of what will be with you and me.

         G      C        Am      D
I still    can see things hopeful-ly.
```

```
                  G   C   Am
Chorus 1    But you,

            D            G      C   Am
            Why you wanna give me a runa-round?

            D       G  C     Am        D
            Is it a sure - fire__ way to speed things up?

               G        C      Am  D   G   C  Am   D
            When all it does is slow_____me down.
```

```
                  G    C        Am  D
Verse 2     And shake me and my confi-dence

                    G    C         Am  D
            About a great many things,

                     G      C    Am  D
            But I've been__ there, I can see it cower

               G            C         Am    D
            Like a nervous magician waiting in the wings

               G   C        Am        D
            Of a bad play where the heroes are right
```

```
    G        C           Am      D
And nobody thinks or ex-pects too much.

    G           C            Am      D
And Hollywood's calling for the movie rights,

        G            C      Am     D
Singing, "Hey, babe, let's keep in touch."

      G       C     Am       D
Hey, ba-by, let's keep in touch."

            G          C            Am              D
But I want more than a touch, I want you to reach me

    G              C            Am       D
And show me all the things no one else can see.

    G       C          Am     D
So what you feel becomes mine as well.

    G                 C           Am     D
And soon, if we're luck-y, we'd be un-able to tell

        G         C       Am      D
What's yours and mine, the fishing's fine,

            G        C                Am        D
And it does-n't have to rhyme, so don't you feed me a line.
```

Chorus 2   ***Repeat Chorus 1***

Solo   ‖: G   C   Am| D   :‖   *Play 6 times*

Verse 3
```
       G   C
Tra, la, la bom - ba, dear,

    Am        D
This is the pilot speaking,

        G        C      Am    D
And I've  got some__ news for you.

        G        C
It seems my ship still stands

      Am          D
No mat-ter what you drop,

              G      C      Am    D
And there ain't a whole lot that you can do.

            G        C
Oh, sure, the banner may be torn

      Am          D
And the wind's gotten colder,

G          C            Am      D
     Perhaps I've grown a little cynical,

    G      C              Am      D
But I know no mat-ter what the waitress brings

          G   C      Am        D
I shall drink__ in and always be full.

          G        C      Am        D
Yeah, I will__ drink it and always be full.

    G    C        Am   D
Oh, I like__ coffee and I like tea,

    G    C      Am   D
But to be able to enter a final plea.

    G    C              Am        D
I still got this dream that you just can't shake,

    G        C            Am        D
I love you to the point you can no longer take.

            G C   Am        D
Well, alright,__ okay, so be that way,

    G      C            Am            D
I hope and pray that there's something left to say.
```

                         G   C   Am
Chorus 3   But you,

               D   G   C   Am
               Why you wanna give me a runa-round?

               D   G   C   Am   D
               Is it a sure - fire__ way to speed things up?

                     G   C   Am   D
               When all it does is slow me down.

                     G   C   Am
               Oh, you.

               D   G   C   Am
               Why you wanna give me a runa-round?

               D   G   C   Am   D
               Is it a sure - fire__ way to speed things up?

                     G   C   Am D   G   C   Am   D
               When all it does is slow_____me down.

Outro   ‖: G   C   Am| D   :‖   *Repeat and fade*

GUITAR CHORD SONGBOOK

Show Me the Way

Words and Music by Peter Frampton

I won - der how you're feel - ing,

D	Dmaj7	Bm	B♭	C	A7sus4	G	G/A
1 3 2	1 1 1	1 3 4 2 1	1 3 3 3	1 3 3 3	1 3	2 1 3	3 4 2 1

Intro   ‖: D | Dmaj7 | Bm | B♭   C   :‖   *Play 4 times*

Verse 1
       D
I wonder how you're feeling,

         Dmaj7
There's   ringing in my ears,

     Bm
And no one to relate to

           B♭   **C**
'Cept the sea.

 D
Who can I believe in?

    Dmaj7
I'm   kneeling on the floor.

     Bm
There has to be a force,

      B♭
Who do__ I phone?

Bridge 1

       A7sus4
The stars around me shining,

       G
But all I really want to know...

Chorus 1

       Bm
Oh, won't you

       G
Show me the way,

Ev'ry day.

       Bm
I want you

       G   **G/A**
To show me the way, yeah.

Interlude 1 | D | Dmaj7 | Bm | Bb   C |

Verse 2

       D
Well, I can see no reason,

       Dmaj7
Your living on your nerves,

       Bm
When someone drops a cup,

       Bb   **C**
And I__ submerge.

       D
I'm swimming in a circle,

       Dmaj7
I   feel I'm going down.

       Bm
There has to be a fool

       Bb
To play__ my part.

Bridge 2

    A7sus4
Someone thought of healing

      G
But all I really want to know...

Chorus 2

       Bm
Oh, won't you

     G
Show me the way,

Ev'ry day.

    Bm
I want you

    G
To show me the way, oh.

    Bm
I want you

    G   **G/A**
Day after day,   hey.

Solo

D		Dmaj7		
Bm		Bb		C
D		Dmaj7		
Bm		G		

Verse 3

        D
And I wonder if I'm dreaming,

    Dmaj7
I   feel so unashamed.

    Bm   **Bb**
I can't believe this is happening to me.

Bridge 3

    A7sus4
I watch you when you're sleeping,

       G
Oh, then I___ wanna take your love...

Chorus 3

      Bm
Oh, won't you

       G
Show me the way,

Ev'ry day.

     Bm
I want you

       G
To show me the way,

One more time.

     Bm
I want you

   G
Day after day, hey.

     Bm
I want you

    G   **G/A**
Day after day,   hey.

Interlude 2 | D | Dmaj7 | Bm | G |

                                  Bm
Chorus 4   I want you

                          G
              To show me the way

              Ev'ry day.

                          Bm
              I want you

                          G
              To show me the way

              Night and day.

                          Bm
              I want you

                      G   G/A
              Day after day,

                      D
              Hey, hey,

                  Dmaj7   Bm   Bb C   D
              Oh.

Seven Bridges Road

Words and Music by Stephen T. Young

Verse 1

N.C.
There are stars in the southern sky,

Southward as you go.

There is moonlight and moss in the trees

Down the Seven Bridges Road.

Interlude

| D | | C | |
| G/B | D | | |

Verse 2
```
        D     C    G/B        D
Now I have loved you like a ba - by,
              C         G/B   D
Like some lonesome child.
                C    G/B        D
And I have loved you in a tame ___ way,
              C    G/B  D
And I have loved wild.
```

Bridge
```
                C                D
Some-times there's a part ___ of me
                C                D
Has to turn from here and go.
C                        D
Runnin' like a child from these warm stars
                  C       G/B  D
Down the Seven Bridges Road.
```

Verse 3
```
            N.C.
There are stars in the southern sky,

And if ever you decide you should go,

There is a taste of time sweet and honey

Down the Seven Bridges Road.
```

Silent Lucidity

Words and Music by Chris DeGarmo

Melody:

Hush   now,   don't _   you   cry, _____

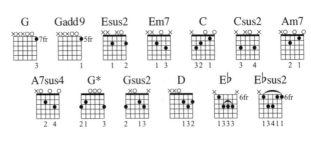

G	Gadd9	Esus2	Em7	C	Csus2	Am7

A7sus4	G*	Gsus2	D	E♭	E♭sus2

Intro

| G   Gadd9 | G   Gadd9 | Esus2   Em7 |

| Esus2   Em7 |

Verse 1

G   Gadd9   G
  Hush now, don't you cry,

Gadd9   Esus2   Em7   Esus2   Em7
Wipe away the tear - drop from your eye.

G   Gadd9   G
  You're lying safe in bed,

    Gadd9   Esus2   Em7   Esus2   Em7
It was all a bad dream spinning in your head.

C   Csus2   C
  Your mind tricked you to feel the pain

   Csus2   Am7
Of someone close to you

          A7sus4   Am7   A7sus4
Leaving the game   of life.

C   Csus2   C
  So here it is, ___ another chance,

Csus2   Am7
Wide awake you face ___ the day,

   A7sus4
Your dream is over…or has it just begun?

| G*   Gsus2 | G*   Gsus2 | Esus2 Em7 |
                    | Esus2 Em7 |

erse 2
          G*   Gsus2   G*
          There's a place I like to hide,

          Gsus2   Esus2   Em7   Esus2   Em7
          A doorway that I run through in the night.

          G*   Gsus2   G
          Relax, child, you were there,

              Gsus2   Esus2   Em7   Esus2   Em7
          But only didn't realize it, and you were scared.

          C   Csus2   C   Csus2
              It's a place where you will learn ___ to face your fears,

              Am7   A7sus4   Am7   A7sus4
          Re-trace the years and ride the whims of your mind.

          C   Csus2   C
              Commanding in another world,

          Csus2   Am7   A7sus4   Am7   A7sus4
          Suddenly, you hear and see this magic new dimen - sion.

horus 1
          D   C
          (I…) _____   Will be watching over you.

          D   C
          (I…) _____   Am gonna help to see it through.

          D   C
          (I…) _____   Will protect you in the night.

          D   Csus2
          (I…) _____   Am smiling next to you,

                  G   Gadd9   G   Gadd9
          In silent lucidity.

Guitar Solo | Eb   Ebsus2 | Eb   Ebsus2 | Csus2 C |
                | Csus2 C | Eb   Ebsus2 | Eb   Ebsus2 |
                | Csus2 C | N.C.(C/Bb) | N.C.(Ab) |
                | (G) | (F) | (Eb) |
                | (D) | (C) | (Bb) |
                | (Ab) | (G) | |

Verse 3

  G* Gsus2   G*
  If you open your mind for me,

  Gsus2 Esus2   Em7 Esus2 Em7
You won't rely on open eyes to see.

  G*   Gsus2 G*
  The walls you built within,

   Gsus2   Esus2   Em7 Esus2 Em7
Come tumbling down and a new world will begin.

 C Csus2   C
  Living twice at once, you learn

  Csus2   Am7
You're safe from pain in the dream domain.

 A7sus4   Am7 A7sus4
A soul set free to fly.

 C   Csus2   C
  A round-trip journey in your head,

 Csus2 Am7   A7sus4
Master of illu - sion, can you realize

  Am7   A7sus4
Your dream's alive, you can be the guide but...

Chorus 2

 D C
 (I...) _____ Will be watching over you.

 D C
 (I...) _____ Am gonna help to see it through.

 D C
 (I...) _____ Will protect you in the night.

 D Csus2
 (I...) _____ Am smiling next to you.

Outro

 ‖: G Gadd9 :‖ *Play 5 times*
 | G

Space Oddity

Words and Music by David Bowie

Ground Con - trol __ to Ma - jor Tom. __

Intro	‖: **Fmaj7♯11/E**　　　|**Em**　　　:‖	***Play 4 times***

Verse 1

  C   **Em**
  Ground Control to Major Tom.

  C   **Em**
  Ground Control to Major Tom.

  Am **Am/G** **D/F♯**
  Take your protein pills and put your helmet on.

Verse 2

  C   **Em**
  Ground Control to Major Tom,

  C   **Em**
  Commencing countdown; engines on.

  Am **Am/G** **D/F♯**
  Check ig-nition and may God's love be with you.

  \|**N.C.** \| \| \|

Chorus 1

```
C                                    E7
This is Ground Control to Major Tom,

                                 F
You've really made the grade

      Fm               C                      F
And the papers want to know ___ whose shirts you wear.

      Fm            C            F
Now it's time to leave the capsule if you dare.

C                                    E7
This is Major Tom to Ground Control,

                               F
I'm stepping through the door

      Fm               C            F
And I'm floating in a most ___ a peculiar way

            Fm          C         F
And the stars ___ look very different today.
```

Bridge 1

```
      Fmaj7♯11  Em
For here am I   sitting in a tin can,

Fmaj7♯11         Em
Far above the world.

B♭           Am*              G              F
Planet Earth is blue and there's nothing I can do.
```

Interlude 1

```
| C*  F  G  A | C*  F  G  A | Fmaj7♯11         |
| Em7         | A*          | C                |
| D/E         | E5          |                  |
```

Chorus 2

```
            C                                    E7
            Though I'm past one hundred thousand miles
                            F
            I'm feeling very still
                Fm              C              F
            And I think my spaceship knows which way to go.
                    Fm          C              F
            Tell my wife I love her very much. She knows.
            G           E
            Ground Control to Major Tom,
                Am                  Am/G
            Your circuit's dead, there's something wrong.
                    D/F♯
            Can you hear me, Major Tom?
                    C                   Cadd2/G
            Can you hear me, Major Tom?
                    G*
            Can you hear me, Major Tom?

            Can you…
```

Bridge 2

```
            Fmaj7♯11    Em
            Here am I    floating 'round my tin can,
            Fmaj7♯11            Em
            Far above the moon.
            B♭         Am*             G           F
            Planet Earth is blue and there's nothing I can do.
```

Interlude 2

```
            │C* F  G  A │C* F  G  A │ Fmaj7♯11         │
            │Em7        │A*         │ C                │
            │D/E        │           │                  │
```

Outro

```
            ‖: E5*          │                   :‖  Repeat and fade
```

Somebody to Love

Words and Music by Darby Slick

Verse 1

     F#m   **B**
When the truth is found

Esus4 F#m
To be_____ lies,

       B
And all the joy

  Esus4 F#m
With-in you_____ dies,

Chorus 1

N.C. **A**   **E**   **F#m**
Don't you want some-body to love?

B   **A**   **E**   **F#m**
Don't you need some-body to love?

B   **A**   **E**   **F#m**
Wouldn't you love some-body to love?

B   **A**   **B**   **F#m**
You better find__ some-body to love.

Interlude 1 | **B** | **F#m**   **E** | **F#m** | |

Verse 2

     F#m   **B**
When the garden's flowers,

  Esus4 **F#m**
Ba - by, are____ dead,

Yes, and your mind,

     B E **F#m**
Your mind__ is so full of red.

Chorus 2   *Repeat Chorus 1*

                         F#m
Verse 3   Your eyes,

          I say your eyes may look like his.

                              B
          Yeah, but in your head, baby,

                         F#m
          I'm afraid you don't know where it is.

Chorus 3   *Repeat Chorus 1*

Interlude 2 | E | B   A | | F#m | |

          F#m   B
Verse 4   Tears are running,

                  F#m   B   E
          They're all run - ning down your breast,

            F#m   B
          And your friends, baby,

             E   F#m
          They treat you like a guest.

Chorus 4   *Repeat Chorus 1*

Outro | F#m | B | | |
            | F#m | E | F#m | B   E |
            | F#m | B E | F#m | B   E |
            | F#m | | A E | B |
            | A E | B | A E | B | A B |

Someday I'll Be Saturday Night

Words and Music by Desmond Child,
Jon Bon Jovi and Richie Sambora

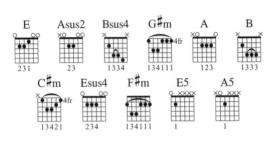

Intro

E
Hey, man, I'm alive,

Asus2
I'm tak - ing each day a night at a time.

Bsus4
I'm feeling like a Monday,

                              E
But someday I'll be Saturday ___ night.

Verse 1

E
Hey, my name is Jim, where did I go wrong?

G♯m
My life's a bargain basement, all the good shit's gone.

A
I just can't hold a job. And where do I belong?

E   **Bsus4**   **E**
Been sleeping in my car, my dreams move on.

Verse 2

E
My name is Billy Jean, my love is bought and sold.

G#m
I'm only sixteen; I feel a hundred years old.

A
My foster daddy went, took my innocence away.

B   Bsus4   B
The street life ain't much better but at least I'm get-ting paid.

Pre-Chorus 1

C#m   A
And Tuesday just might come ____ my way.

E   Esus4   E
It can't get worse than yes-terday.

G#m
Thursdays, Fridays, ain't been kind.

A   F#m
But somehow I've survived.

Chorus 1

E
Hey, man, I'm alive,

A
I'm tak - ing each day a night at a time.

E   Bsus4
Yeah, I'm down, but I know I'll get by.

B Bsus4   B   A   B
   Hey, hey,   hey, hey ____ man, gotta live my life

E   C#m
Like I ain't got nothing but this roll of the dice.

Bsus4   B
I'm feeling like a Monday,

Asus2   E   A
But some - day I'll be Saturday ____ night.

Verse 3

      E
Now, I can't say my name or tell you where I am.

      G♯m
I wanna blow myself away, don't know if I can.

   A
I wish that I could be in some other time and place.

   B   Bsus4   B
With someone else's soul, some - one else's face.

Pre-Chorus 2

    C♯m   A
Or Tuesday just might come ___ my way.

  E   Esus4 E
It can't get worse than yes-terday.

G♯m
Thursdays, Fridays, ain't been kind.

   A   F♯m
But somehow I've survived.

Chorus 2

  E
Hey, man, I'm alive,

     A
I'm tak - ing each day a night at a time.

  E   Bsus4
Yeah, I'm down, but I know I'll get by.

 B Bsus4   B   A   B
  Hey, hey,   hey, hey ___ man, gotta live my life

      E   C♯m
Like I ain't got nothing but this roll of the dice.

   Bsus4   B
I'm feeling like a Monday,

     Asus2   E
But some - day I'll be Saturday ___ night.

Guitar Solo

| A | | E | | |
| A | | E | E5 | |

Ooh.

| A5 | | E | E5 | |

Saturday night.

| A5 | | |

                E5
Bridge   Someday I'll be Saturday night.

                    A5
            I'll be back on my feet. I'll be doing alright.

                E5
            It may not be tomorrow, baby; that's o.k.

                    A5
            I ain't going down, gonna find a way. Hey, hey, hey.

                E
Chorus 3 Hey, man, I'm alive,

                    A
            I'm tak - ing each day a night at a time.

                E   Bsus4
            Yeah, I'm down, but I know I'll get by.

            B Bsus4 B   A   B
                Hey, hey,   hey, hey ___ man, gotta live my life

                        E   C#m
            Like I ain't got nothing but this roll of the dice.

                    Bsus4   B
            I'm feeling like a Monday,

                        Asus2   E
            But some - day I'll be Saturday ___ night.

                        B
            Oh, I'm feeling like a Monday,

                        A   E
            But some - day I'll be Saturday night.

Outro   ‖: A | | E | :‖ *Repeat and fade*
                                             (w/voc. ad lib.)

ACOUSTIC ROCK   **179**

The Sound of Silence

Words and Music by Paul Simon

Melody:

Hel-lo dark-ness, my old friend,

(Capo 4th fret)

Verse 1

   Bsus2   **A**
   Hello darkness, my old friend,

                    Bsus2
   I've come to talk with you a-gain.

                G   **D**
   Because a vision softly ___ creeping,

                G   **D**
   Left it's seeds while I was ____ sleeping.

     G   **D**
   And the vision that was planted in my brain

           Bm D   **A**   **Bm**
   Still remains   within the sound of silence.

Verse 2

                   A
   In restless dreams I walked a-lone

                Bm
   Narrow streets of cobble-stone.

              G   **D**
   'Neath the halo of a ___ streetlamp

              G   **D**
   I turned my collar to the cold and damp.

      G   **D**
   When my eyes were stabbed by the flash of a neon light

            Bm D   **A**   **Bm**
   That split the night   and touched the sound of silence.

Verse 3

         A
And in the naked light I saw
         Bm
Ten thousand people, maybe more.
         G   **D**
People talking without ___ speaking;
         G   **D**
People hearing without ___ list'ning.
         G   **D**
People writing songs that voices never share.
         Bm D   **A**   **Bm**
And no one dare   disturb the sound of silence.

Verse 4

         A
"Fools!" said I, "You do not know
         Bm
Silence like a cancer grows.
         G   **D**
Hear my words that I might ___ teach you.
         G   **D**
Take my arms that I might ___ reach you."
         G   **D**
But my words like silent raindrops fell,
Bm   **D**   **A**   **Bm**
And echoed in the wells of silence.

Verse 5

         A
And the people bowed and prayed
         Bm
To the neon god they made.
         G   **D**
And the sign flashed out its ___ warning.
         G   **D**
In the words that it was ___ forming.
         G
And the signs said, "The words of the prophets
         D   **Bm**
Are written on the subway walls ___ and tenement halls."
D   **A**   **Bm**
Whisper the sounds of silence.

Strong Enough

Words and Music by Kevin Gilbert,
David Baerwald, Sheryl Crow, Brian McLeod,
Bill Bottrell and David Ricketts

Melody:

God, I feel __ like hell __ to - night.

D   G5   Bmb6   A   Em   G   Bm   C

Intro

‖: D   G5 |Bmb6   A   :‖   *Play 4 times*

Verse 1

D   G5   Bmb6   A
God, I feel like hell ____ to-night.

D   G5   Bmb6   A
Tears of rage I can - not fight.

            D   G5   Bmb6
I'll be the last to help you un - der-stand.

A   D   G5   Bmb6
Are you strong enough to be ____ my man?

A   D   G5   Bmb6   A
My ____ man.

Interlude 1   ‖: **D**   **G5** |**Bm♭6**   **A**   :‖ *Play 3 times*

Verse 2

D   **G5** **Bm♭6** **A**
Nothing's true and noth - ing's right.

   D   **G5**   **Bm♭6** **A**
Just let me be alone ____ to-night,

      D   **G5**   **Bm♭6**
'Cause you can't change the way ____ I am.

A   **D**   **G5**   **Bm♭6** **A**
Are you strong enough to be ____ my man?

Chorus 1

Em D   **G**   **A**
Lie ____ to me,

 Bm   **C**   **G**   **A**
I promise, I believe.

Em D   **G**   **A**
Lie ____ to me,

   Bm   **C** **G** **A**
But please, don't leave.

Interlude 2 | **D**   **G5** |**Bm♭6**   **A** |
                             Don't leave.

               ‖: **D**   **G5** |**Bm♭6**   **A** :‖ *Play 3 times*

Verse 3

   D   **G5**   **Bm♭6**   **A**
I have a face I can - not show.

   D   **G5**   **Bm♭6**   **A**
I make the rules up as ____ I go.

     D   **G5**   **Bm♭6**
Just try and love me if ____ you can.

A   **D**   **G5**   **Bm♭6**   **A**
Are you strong enough to be ____ my man?

   D   **G5**   **Bm♭6**
My ____ man.

A   **D**   **G5**   **Bm♭6**
Are you strong enough to be my man?

A   **D**   **G5**   **Bm♭6**
Are you strong enough to be my man?

A   **D**   **G5**   **Bm♭6**   **A**
Are you strong enough to be ____ my man?

Verse 4

         D   **G5**   **Bm♭6**   **A**
Now when I show you that I just ____ don't care,

         D   **G5**   **Bm♭6**   **A**
When I'm throwing punches in ____ the air,

         D   **G5**   **Bm♭6**
When I'm broken down and I ____ can't stand,

      A   **D**   **G5**   **Bm♭6**   **A**
Would you be man enough to be ____ my man?

Chorus 2

Em D   **G**   **A**
Lie ____ to me,

 Bm   **C**   **G**   **A**
I promise, I believe.

Em D   **G**   **A**
Lie ____ to me,

   Bm   **C**   **G**   **A**
But please, don't leave.

Sweet Jane

Words and Music by Lou Reed

Stand - ing on the cor - ner,

D A Bm G
1333 134211 134111 134211

Intro

‖: D   A |Bm G A |D   A |Bm A G A :‖

Verse 1

D A   G   Bm   A D
Standing on the corner,

    A   G   Bm   A D
Suit-case in my hand.

                   A   G   Bm   A D
Jack is in his corset, Jane is in her vest,

                  A   G Bm A D
And me I'm in a rock and roll band.   Huh.

A   G   Bm   A D
Ridin' in a Stutz Bearcat, Jim,

       A   G   Bm A D
You know those were diff'rent __ times.

     A   G   Bm
Oh, all the poets, they studied rules of verse,

A   D   A   G Bm A D
And those ___ ladies, they rolled their eyes.

ACOUSTIC ROCK

Chorus 1

                 D   G   A   D
            Sweet Jane, ____ whoa.

                         G A   D
      Sweet Jane, _____ oh, oh.

                         G   A   D
      Sweet Jane.

Verse 2

                 D   A   G   Bm A D
          I'll tell you something, Jack, he is a banker,

                         A G   Bm A   D
    And Jane, _____ she is a clerk.

                         A   G   Bm   A   D
    And both of them save their monies,

                                  A   G   Bm A   D
    Ha, and when, when they come home from work.

                    A   G   Bm A D
    Ooh, sittin' down by the fire, ____ oh,

                        A   G   Bm A   D
    The radi-o does ___ play   the clas-sical music there, Jim,

                        A   G   Bm
    "The March of the Wooden Sol-diers."

                 A   D   A   G   Bm A   D
    All you pro-test kids, you can hear Jack ___ say,   get ready, ah.

Chorus 2   *Repeat Chorus 1*

Verse 3

      D A   **G**   **Bm**   **A**   **D**
Some peo-ple, they like to go out dancing,

          A   **G**   **Bm**   **A**   **D**
And other peo-ples, they have to work. Just watch me, now.

            A   **G**   **Bm** **A**   **D**
And there's even some evil mothers,

                    A G   **Bm**   **A**   **D**
Well, they're gonna tell you that   ev'rything is just ___ dirt.

           A **G**   **Bm** **A**   **D**
Y'know that wom - en never really faint, and that

         A   **G**   **Bm** **A**   **D**
Villains always blink their eyes, woo,

           A   **G**   **Bm**   **A**   **D**
And that, y'know, ___ children are the only ones who blush,

          A G   **Bm** **A**   **D**
And that life is just to die.

         A   **G**   **Bm** **A**   **D**
But anyone who ever had a heart,

         A   **G**   **Bm** **A**   **D**
Oh, they wouldn't turn around and break it.

         A   **G** **Bm** **A**   **D**
And anyone who ever played a part,

         A   **G**   **Bm** **A**   **D**
Oh, they wouldn't turn around and hate it.

Chorus 3

D   **G**   **A** **D**
Sweet Jane, __ oh, whoa.

         G   **A**   **D**
Sweet Jane.

       G
Sweet Jane.   Sweet Jane.

Outro

     D   **G**   **A**
‖: Sweet Jane. Sweet Jane. :‖

Suite: Judy Blue Eyes

Words and Music by Stephen Stills

Melody:

Open E5 tuning:
(low to high) E–E–E–E–B–E

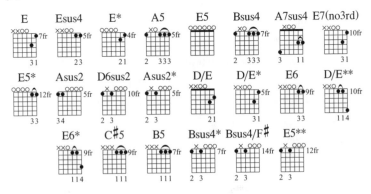

Intro

```
|E          |    Esus4|E*    |          |          |
|E          |    Esus4|E*    |          |
```

Verse 1

                     A5
It's getting to the point

            E5   **Bsus4**
Where I'm no fun anymore.

       A5 **A7sus4**
I am sorry.

E5   **A5**
   Sometimes it hurts

         E5   **Bsus4**
So badly I must cry out loud.

      A5   **A7sus4**
I am lonely.

Chorus 1

            E5   **Bsus4**
I am yours, ___ you are mine,

            A5   **A7sus4**
You are what ___ you are.

          E5   **A5**
You make it hard.

Verse 2

   E*   **A5**
Re-member what we've said

          E5   **Bsus4**
And done and felt about each other.

            A5   **A7sus4**
Oh, babe, have mercy.

E5   **A5**
  Don't let the past

         E5   **Bsus4**
Remind us of what we are not now.

       A5   **A7sus4**
I am not dreaming.

Chorus 2

          E5   **Bsus4**
I am yours, ___ you are mine,

        A5   **A7sus4**
You are what you are.

        E5
You make it hard.

Interlude 1

| **E** | | | **Esus4** | **E*** | | |

                           Oh, _____ oh, oh.

| **E** | **E7(no3rd)** | **E** | **Esus4** | **E*** | |

Verse 3

```
E*              A5
     Tearing yourself
                E5         Bsus4
Away from me now, you are free,
          A5     A7sus4
And I am crying.
E5              A5
     This does not mean
                     E5
I don't love you, I do,
          Bsus4
That's for-ever,
             A5     A7sus4
Yes, and for always.
```

Chorus 3   *Repeat Chorus 1*

Verse 4

```
E*              A5
     Something inside
                E5         Bsus4
Is telling me that I've got your secret.
          A5       A7sus4
Are you still list'ning?
E5              A5
     Fear is the lock
                E5         Bsus4
And laughter the key to your heart.
          A5     A7sus4
And I love you.
```

Chorus 4

          E5   **Bsus4**
I am yours, ___ you are mine,

            A5   **A7sus4**
You are what ___ you are.

      E5   **A5**
You make it hard.

         E5   **A5**
And you make it hard.

         E5   **A5**
And you make it hard.

         E5
And you make it hard.

Interlude 2 | **E5***   **Esus4 E*** | **E5***   **Esus4 E*** |

Bridge 1

E5*   **Esus4 E***   **E5***   **Esus4 E***
 Fri   -   day eve - ning,

E5* **Esus4 E***   **Asus2**   **A7sus4**
 Sun-day in ___ the af - ternoon.

             E5*   **Esus4 E* E5***   **Esus4 E***
What have you got to lose?

Bridge 2

E5*   **Esus4 E***   **E5***   **Esus4 E***
 Tues -   day morn - ing,

E5*   **Esus4 E***   **Asus2**   **A7sus4**
 Please be gone, ___ I'm tired of you.

             E5*   **Esus4 E* E5***   **Esus4 E***
What have you got to lose?

   D6sus2
Can I tell it like it is?

   Asus2*
But listen to me, baby.

D6sus2   **Asus2***
 It's my heart that's a suff'rin', it's a dyin'.

            E5*   **Esus4 E* E5***
That's what I have to lose.

Bridge 3

E5*   Esus4 E*   E5*   Esus4 E*
I've _____ got an an - swer,

E5*   Esus4 E* Asus2   A7sus4
I'm go - ing to fly away.

                    E5*   Esus4 E* E5*   Esus4 E*
What have I got to lose?

Bridge 4

E5*   Esus4 E*   E5*   Esus4 E*
Will _____ you come see me

E5*   Esus4   E* Asus2   A7sus4
Thurs-days and ___ Saturdays? Hey, (hey,) hey.

                    E5*   Esus4 E* E5*
What have you got to lose?

Guitar Solo 1

‖: E5 | | | :‖ *Play 4 times*
| | |

Verse 5

D/E   E*
Chestnut brown canar - y,

D/E   Esus4 E*
Ruby throated spar   -   row,

D/E*   E   E6   E7(no3rd)
Sing a song,   don't be long,

                      D/E** E6*
Thrill me to the mar   -   row.

Guitar Solo 2

‖: E5 | | | :‖
| |

Verse 6

D/E   E*
Voices of the an - gels,

D/E   Esus4 E*
Ring around the moon   -   light,

D/E*   E   E6   E7(no3rd)
Asking me, said she so free,

                      D/E** E6*
"How can you catch the spar   -   row?"

Guitar Solo 3 ‖: E5 | | | :‖
| |

Verse 7
    D/E   **E***   **Esus4 E***
    Lacy, lilting lyr - ic,
    D/E   **Esus4 E***
    Losing love, lament   -   ing,
    D/E*   **E**   **E7(no3rd)**
    Change my life, make it right,
          D/E** **E6***
    Be my la   -   dy.

Interlude 3
| **D/E**** | **E6*** | **D/E**** | **E6*** |
| **D/E**** **E6*** **D/E**** | **E6*** **D/E**** | **E6*** **C♯5** | **B5** |

Outro
    N.C.
‖: Do, do, do, do, do,

Do, do, do, do, do, do.

Do, do, do, do, do,

Do, do, do, do. :‖

‖: **Asus2***   **Bsus4***   **Bsus4/F♯**   **D6sus2**   **E5*** :‖ *Play 8 times*

Asus2*   **Bsus4***   **Bsus4/F♯** **D6sus2**   **E5***
Do, do, do, do, do,   do,   do, do, do, do, do.

Asus2*   **Bsus4***   **Bsus4/F♯** **D6sus2** **E5***
Do, do, do, do, do,   do,   do,   do, do.

Asus2*   **Bsus4***   **Bsus4/F♯** **D6sus2**   **E5***
Do, do, do, do, do,   do,   do, do, do, do, do.

Asus2*   **Bsus4***   **Bsus4/F♯** **D6sus2 E**
Do, do, do, do, do,   do,   do,   do, do.

Sweet Talkin' Woman

Words and Music by Jeff Lynne

Melody:

Sweet talk - in' wom - an,

| F | G | Am | C | Em | A | Dm | Em7 |

Intro

| F G |Am |F G |C |
F G   Am   F   G   C
Sweet talkin' woman, where did you go?

Verse 1

       C
I was searchin' (Searchin'.) on a one way street.

       Am   F
I was hopin' (Hopin'.) for a chance to meet.

       Em   A
I was waitin' for the opera - tor on the line.

Pre-Chorus 1

Dm   Em   Dm
  (She's gone so ____ long.) What can I do?

                    Em
(Where could she ____ be?) No, no, no.

F   G   Am
Don't know what I'm gonna do,

  F   G   C   G
I gotta get back ____ to you.

          C
You gotta slow down, (Slow down.)

Am   **Em**
Sweet talkin' woman. (Slow down.)

F   **Em7**
  You got me runnin', (Run, run.)

F   **G**
  You got me searchin'.

C   **Am**   **Em**
Hold on, (Hold on.) sweet talkin' lover. (Hold on.)

F   **Em7**   **F**   **G**
  It's so sad if that's __ the way it's over.

F **G** **Am**   **F**
Sweet talkin' woman.

Verse 2

     G **C**
I was…(Walkin'.) Many days go by.

      Am   **F**
I was thinkin' (Thinkin'.) 'bout the lonely nights.

      Em   **A**
Com-munication break - down all around.

Pre-Chorus 2   *Repeat Pre-Chorus 1*

Chorus 2

          C
You gotta slow down, (Slow down.)

Am   **Em**
Sweet talkin' woman. (Slow down.)

F   **Em7**
  You got me runnin', (Run, run.)

F   **G**
  You got me searchin'.

C   **Am**   **Em**
Hold on, (Hold on.) sweet talkin' lover. (Hold on.)

F   **Em7**   **F**   **G**
  It's so sad if that's __ the way it's over.

F **G** **Am**
Sweet talkin' woman.

Verse 3

         C
I've been livin' (Livin'.) on a dead end street.

       Am   **F**
I've been askin' (Kindly.) ev'ry-body I meet.

Em   **A**
Insufficient da - ta comin' through.

Pre-Chorus 3   *Repeat Pre-Chorus 1*

Chorus 3

          C
You gotta slow down, (Slow down.)

Am   **Em**
Sweet talkin' woman. (Slow down.)

F   **Em7**
  You got me runnin', (Run, run.)

F   **G**
  You got me searchin'.

C   **Am**   **Em**
Hold on, (Hold on.) sweet talkin' lover. (Hold on.)

F   **Em7**   **F**   **G**
  It's so sad if that's __ the way it's over.

F   **G**   **Am**   **G**
Sweet talkin' woman.

Chorus 4

C   **Am**   **Em**
Slow down, (Slow down.) sweet talkin' woman. (Slow down.)

F   **Em7** **F**   **G**
  You got me runnin', you got me searchin'.

C   **Am**   **Em**
Hold on, (Hold on.) sweet talkin' lover. (Hold on.)

F   **Em7**   **F**   **G**
  It's so sad if that's __ the way it's over.

Outro-Chorus   *Repeat Chorus 4 till fade*

Tangled Up in Blue

Words and Music by Bob Dylan

Melody:

Ear - ly one morn-in' the sun __ was shin-in', __

A   Asus4   G/A   D   E   F#m   G

Intro

‖: A   Asus4 | A   Asus4 :‖

Verse 1

   A   G/A   A   G/A
Early one mornin' the sun ____ was shinin', I was lay'n' in bed,

   A   G/A   D
Wond'rin' if she'd changed at all, if her hair was still red.

   A   G/A   A   G/A
Her folks, they said our lives ____ together sure was gonna be rough.

       A   G/A
They never did like Mama's homemade dress,

      D
Papa's bank book wasn't big enough.

     E   F#m   A   D
And I was standin' on the side of the road, rain ____ fallin' on my shoes.

 E   F#m
   Heading up for the East ____ Coast,

     A   D   E
Lord knows I've paid some dues ____ gettin' through;

 G   D   A
Tangled up in blue.

Interlude 1   *Repeat Intro*

Verse 2

   A   G/A   A   G/A
She was married when we ___ first met,   soon to be divorced.

   A   G/A   D
   I helped her out of a jam, ___ I guess, but I used a little too much force.

     A   G/A   A   G/A
We drove that car as far as we could, a-bandoned it out West,

   A   G/A   D
   Split up on a dark ___ sad night, both a-greeing it was best.

     E   F♯m   A   D
As she turned around to look at me as I ___ was a walkin' away,

   E   F♯m
   I heard her say over my ___ shoulder,

              A   D   E
"We'll meet ___ again someday ___ on the avenue."

   G   D   A
Tangled up in blue.

Interlude 2   *Repeat Intro*

Verse 3

   A   G/A   A   G/A
I had a job in the great north woods, working as a cook for a spell.

     A   G/A   D
But I never did like it all ___ that much and one day the axe just fell.

     A   G/A   A   G/A
So I drifted down to New Orleans where I lucky was to be em-ployed.

   A   G/A   D
Workin' for a while on a fishin' boat right out - side of Delacroix.

   E   F♯m   A   D
But all the while I was alone, the past ___ was close behind.

   E   F♯m
I seen a lot of women,

       A   D   E
But she never escaped my mind, ___ and I just grew

   G   D   A
Tangled up in blue.

Interlude 3   *Repeat Intro*

Verse 4

```
A                G/A              A                    G/A
She was workin' in a topless place and I __ stopped in for a beer.

A                  G/A              D
I just kept lookin' at the side of her face in the spotlight so clear.

A                G/A              A                    G/A
And later on when the crowd thinned out, I's just about to do the same.

     A              G/A
She was standin' there in back of my chair,

     D
Said to me, "Don't I know your name?"

E                        F♯m
I muttered somethin' under-neath my breath,

     A                D
She studied the lines on my face.

     E              F♯m
I must admit I felt a little uneasy

          A                  D              E
When she bent down to tie the laces ____ of my shoe;

G     D    A
Tangled up in blue.
```

Interlude 4   *Repeat Intro*

Verse 5

```
        A               G/A            A          G/A
She lit a burner on ___ the stove and offered me a pipe.

        A                       G/A
"I thought you'd never say hel-lo," she said,

        D
"You look like the silent type."

                A       G/A           A         G/A
Then she opened up a book of poems and handed it to me,

A          G/A              D
Written by an I-talian poet from the thirteenth century.

        E                    F♯m
And ev'ry one of them words ___ rang true

             A              D
And glowed __ like burnin' coal.

E           F♯m
Pourin' off of ev'ry page

        A                D              E
Like it was written in my soul from me to you;

G       D       A
Tangled up in blue.
```

Interlude 5   *Repeat Intro*

Verse 6

```
           A           G/A       A              G/A
I lived with them on Montague Street in a basement down the stairs.
           A        G/A       D
There was music in the ca-fés at night and revo-lution in the air.
           A        G/A
Then he started into dealin' with slaves
           A                G/A
And something inside of him died.
           A        G/A            D
She had to sell ev'rything ____ she owned and ____ froze up inside.
           E        F#m          A           D
And when it finally, the bottom fell out I __ became with-drawn.
           E              F#m
The only thing I knew how to do
           A        D           E
Was to keep on keepin' on like a bird that flew;
           G    D    A
Tangled up in blue.
```

Interlude 6   *Repeat Intro*

Verse 7

```
           A           G/A       A              G/A
So now I'm goin' back again, I got to get to her some-how.
           A        G/A         D
All the people we used to know, they're an il-lusion to me now.
           A        G/A    A        G/A
Some are mathema-ticians; some are carpenter's wives.
           A                G/A
Don't know how it all got started,
                 D
I don't know what they're doin' with their lives.
           E        F#m         A              D
But me, I'm still on the road, headin' for another joint.
           E              F#m
We always did feel the same,
           A                D           E
We just saw it from a diff'rent point of view;
           G    D    A
Tangled up in blue.
```

Interlude 7   *Repeat Intro*

Outro   *Repeat Verse 7 (Instrumental)*

Tears in Heaven

Words and Music by
Eric Clapton and Will Jennings

Melody:

Would you know my name

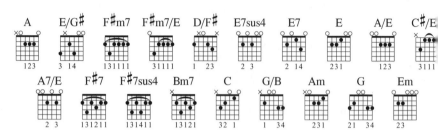

A   E/G♯   F♯m7   F♯m7/E   D/F♯   E7sus4   E7   E   A/E   C♯/E♯

A7/E   F♯7   F♯7sus4   Bm7   C   G/B   Am   G   Em

Intro |A E/G♯ F♯m7 | F♯m7/E | D/F♯   E7sus4 E7| A |

Verse 1

    A   E/G♯   F♯m7 F♯m7/E
    Would you know my name

    D/F♯ A   E A/E E7
    If I saw you in heav-en?

    A   E/G♯ F♯m7   F♯m7/E
    Would it be the same

    D/F♯ A/E   E A/E E7
    If I saw you in heav-en?

Chorus 1

    F♯m7   C♯/E♯
    I must be strong

    A7/E   F♯7
    And carry on,

    F♯7sus4 F♯7   Bm7
    'Cause   I   know

             E7sus4
    I don't belong

            A E/G♯ F♯m7   F♯m7/E D/F♯   E7sus4 E7 A
    Here in heav-en.

```
A           E/G♯   F♯m7    F♯m7/E
  Would you hold my hand
D/F♯   A              E   A/E  E7
  If I saw you in heav-en?
A           E/G♯   F♯m7    F♯m7/E
  Would ya help me stand
D/F♯   A/E            E   A/E  E7
  If I saw you in heav-en?
```

```
F♯m7              C♯/E♯
  I'll find my way
A7/E                    F♯7
  Through night and day
F♯7sus4  F♯7   Bm7
'Cause    I   know
                 E7sus4
I just can't stay
                A   E/G♯  F♯m7     F♯m7/E  D/F♯   E7sus4  E7  A
Here in heav-en.
```

```
C        G/B   Am
  Time can bring ya down,
        D/F♯         G  D/F♯  Em  D/F♯ G
Time can bend your knees.
C        G/B      Am
  Time can break your heart,
        D/F♯       G
Have ya beggin' please,
D/F♯           E   A/E  E7
  Beggin' please.
```

Repeat Verse 2 (Instrumental)

Chorus 3

F#m7   C#/E#
  Beyond the door

A7/E   F#7
  There's peace, I'm sure,

F#7sus4 F#7   Bm7
And   I   know

                  E7sus4
There'll be no more

           A   E/G# F#m7 F#m7/E D/F# E7sus4 E7 A
Tears in heav-en.

Verse 3   *Repeat Verse 1*

Chorus 4

F#m7   C#/E#
  I must be strong

A7/E   F#7
  And carry on,

F#7sus4 F#7   Bm7
'Cause   I   know

               E7sus4
I don't belong

           A   E/G# F#m7
Here in heav-en.

F#m7/E   Bm7
  'Cause I know

               E7sus4
  I don't belong

           A   E/G# F#m7 F#m7/E D/F# E7sus4 E7 A
Here in heav-en.

3 AM

Lyrics by Rob Thomas
Music by Rob Thomas,
Brian Yale, John Leslie Goff
and John Joseph Stanley

Melody:

She says it's cold _____ out - side _ and she hands _ me my rain-

(Capo 1st fret)

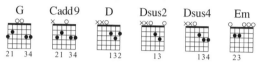

G   Cadd9   D   Dsus2   Dsus4   Em

Intro

| G   Cadd9 | | G   Cadd9 | |

| G   Cadd9 | G   Cadd9 | G   Cadd9 | G   Cadd9 |

Verse 1

    D   Cadd9
She says it's cold ____ outside
                    G
And she hands me my rain - coat.
    D   Cadd9   G   Cadd9   G   Cadd9
She's always worried about things like that.
    D   Cadd9
Well, she says it's all ____ gonna end
                G   Cadd9   G   Cadd9
And it might as well be my ____ fault.
         D   Dsus2   Cadd9
And she only sleeps when it's rain - in'.
      Dsus4   D   Cadd9
And she screams, and her voice ____ is strainin'.

Chorus 1

           G   D   Cadd9
She says, "Baby,   it's three a.m.,
      D   G   D   Cadd9
I __ must be lone - ly."
    D   G   D   Cadd9
When she says, "Baby,   well, I can't help
        D   Em   D
But be scared of it all ____ some-times."
Cadd9
And the rain's gonna wash away, I believe it.

COUSTIC ROCK

Interlude 1   ‖: G   Cadd9 | G   Cadd9 :‖

                D   Cadd9

Verse 2   But she's gotta little ___ bit of somethin',

                          G

       God, it's better than noth - in'.

          D   Cadd9

       And in her color por-trait world

                     G   Cadd9   G   Cadd9

       She believes that she's got it all,   all.

          D   Cadd9

       She swears the moon ___ don't hang

                 G   Cadd9   G   Cadd9

       Quite as high as it used to.

               D   Dsus2   Cadd9

       And she only sleeps when it's rain - in'.

             Dsus4   D   Cadd9

       And she screams, and her voice ___ is strainin'.

                  G   D   Cadd9

Chorus 2   She says, "Baby,   it's three a.m.,

          D   G   D   Cadd9

       I __ must be lone - ly."

       D   G   D   Cadd9

       When she says, "Baby,   well, I can't help

          D   Em   D

       But be scared of it all ___ some-times."

       Cadd9

       And the rain's gonna wash away, I believe, yes

Interlude 2 | G   Cadd9 | G   Cadd9 | G   Cadd9 | G   Cadd9 |

    D   **Cadd9**
Well, she believes ___ that life is made up
               G   **Cadd9** **G** **Cadd9**
Of all that you're used ___ to.
               Cadd9
And the clock on the wall ___ has been stuck at three
   G   **Cadd9**   **G**   **Cadd9**
For days and days.
   D   **Cadd9**
She thinks that hap - piness is a mat
             G **Cadd9**   **G** **Cadd9**
That sits on her door - way,   yeah.
   D   **C**
But outside it stopped rainin'.

           G   **D** **Cadd9**
Yeah, but she says, "Baby,   it's three a.m.,
   D   **G**   **D**   **Cadd9**
I __ must be lone - ly."
D   **G**   **D** **Cadd9**
When she says, "Baby,   well, I can't help
   D   **Em**   **D**
But be scared of it all ___ some-times."
Cadd9
And the rain's gonna wash away,
        G   **D**   **Cadd9**
I believe   this.
              D   **G**   **D** **Cadd9**
Well, it's three a.m., I must be lone - ly.
   D
Whenev-er she says,
G   **D** **Cadd9**
  "Baby,   well, I can't help
     D   **Em** **D** **Cadd9**
But be scared of it all ___ some-times."

Time for Me to Fly

Words and Music by Kevin Cronin

Open D tuning:
(low to high) D-A-D-F#-A-D

Melody:

I've been a - round _ for _ you, I've

D   Aadd4   Gadd9   Gadd9/D   A5

Intro   ‖: D   Gadd9 │ Aadd4   Gadd9   :‖

Verse 1

D
I've been around for you,

    Aadd4
I've been up and down for you,

    Gadd9   D Gadd9/D D Gadd9/D D
But I__ just can't get any relief.

I've swallowed my pride for you,

Aadd4
    Lived and lied for you,

    Gadd9   D Gadd9/D D Gadd9/D D
But a you still make me feel like a thief.

        Aadd4
You got me stealin' your love away

     Gadd9   D
'Cause a you never give it.

Aadd4
Peelin' the years away

    Gadd9   D
And a we can't re-live it.

    Gadd9   D
Oh, I make you laugh,

    Gadd9   D
And a you make me cry.

Aadd4
    I believe it's time for me to fly.

GUITAR CHORD SONGBOO

‖: D   Gadd9 | Aadd4   Gadd9   :‖

Verse 2

D
You said we'd work it out,

Aadd4
You said that you had no doubt,

Gadd9   **D** **Gadd9/D** **D** **Gadd9/D**
That deep down we were really in love.

D
Oh, but I'm tired of holdin' on

Aadd4
To feelin' I know is gone.

Gadd9   **D** **Gadd9/D** **D** **Gadd9/D**
I do believe that I've had enough.

D   **Aadd4**
I've had e-nough of the falseness

Gadd9 **D**
Of a worn - out re-lation.

Aadd4
E-nough of the jealousy

Gadd9 **D**
And the intolera - tion.

Gadd9 **D**
Oh, I make you laugh,

Gadd9   **D**
And a you make me cry.

Aadd4   **D** **Gadd9** **D** **N.C.**
I believe it's time for me to fly.

Chorus 1

                  Aadd4   **Gadd9** **D**
(Time for me to fly.)

        Oh, I've got to set__ myself free.

                  Aadd4   **Gadd9** **D**
(Time for me to fly.)

        Ah, that's just how it's a got to be.

Gadd9   Aadd4
  I know it hurts to say good-bye,

                       Gadd9   Aadd4
But it's time for me to fly.

Interlude | D | | Gadd9| | | |
            | Aadd4 | | D | | |

                     Aadd4   Gadd9   D
Chorus 2   (Time for me to fly.)

                             Oh, I've got to set___ myself free.
                   Aadd4   Gadd9 D
(Time for me to fly.)

                            Ah, that's just how it's a got to   be.
Gadd9   Aadd4
  I know it hurts to say good-bye,

                      Gadd9   Aadd4
But it's time for me to fly.

                Gadd9   A5
It's time for me to fly,___ ee-i, ee-i.

                D
It's time for me to fly.

          Gadd9   Aadd4
(It's time for me to fly.)

          Gadd9   D
It's time for me to fly.

                 Aadd4
(It's time for me to fly.)

          Gadd9   D
It's time for me to fly.

          Gadd9   Aadd4   Gadd9   D
(It's time for me to fly.)

                       Babe,___ it's time for me to fly.

Time in a Bottle

Words and Music by Jim Croce

Melody:

If I could save ___ time in a

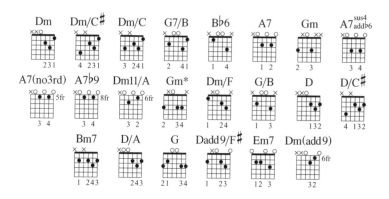

Intro

Dm	Dm/C#	Dm/C	G7/B	
B♭6	A7 Gm	A7 A7sus4add♭6 A7(no3rd)	
A7♭9 Dm11/A A7(no3rd)	

Verse 1

Dm   Dm/C#   Dm/C   G7/B
If I could save ____ time in a bottle,

B♭6   A7 Gm
The first thing that I'd like to do

| A7 A7sus4add♭6 A7(no3rd) | A7♭9 Dm11/A A7(no3rd) |

Dm   Dm/C
Is to save ev'ry-day

B♭6   Gm*   Dm/F
Till e-ternity pass - es away

Gm*   A7 G/B A7(no3rd) A7
Just to spend them with you.

Verse 2

   Dm   **Dm/C♯**   **Dm/C** **G7/B**
If I could make days last for-ever,

   B♭6   **A7 Gm**
If words could make wish-es come

A7 **A7$^{sus4}_{add♭6}$** **A7(no3rd)** **A7♭9** **Dm11/A** **A7(no3rd)**
True;

   Dm   **Dm/C**
I'd save ev'ry-day

   B♭6   **Gm***
Like a treasure and then,

  Dm/F   **Gm***   **A7** **G/B** **A7(no3rd)** **A7**
A-gain I would spend them with you.

Chorus 1

          D   **D/C♯**
But there never seems to be enough time

  Bm7   **D/A**   **G**
To do the things you wanna do once you find them.

| **Dadd9/F♯** | **Em7** | **A7** **G/B** **A7(no3rd)** |

    D   **D/C♯**
I've looked around e-nough to know

  Bm7   **D/A**   **G**
That you're the one I want to go through time with.

| **Dadd9/F♯** | **Em7** | **A7** **G/B** **A7(no3rd)** |

GUITAR CHORD SONGBOOK

Interlude   *Repeat Intro*

Verse 3

    Dm   **Dm/C♯**   **Dm/C** **G7/B**
If I had a box just for wishes,

    B♭6   **A7** **Gm**
And dreams that had never __ come

A7 **A7**$^{\text{sus4}}_{\text{add♭6}}$ **A7(no3rd)** **A7♭9** **Dm11/A** **A7(no3rd)**
True;

    Dm   **Dm/C**
The box would be empty

    B♭6   **Gm***   **Dm/F**
Ex-cept for the mem'ry of how

      Gm*   **A7** **G/B** **A7(no3rd)** **A7**
They were answered by you.

Chorus 2   *Repeat Chorus 1*

Outro   ‖: **Dm(add9)** | :‖ *Play 3 times*

Torn

Words and Music by Phil Thornalley,
Scott Cutler and Anne Previn

I thought I saw _ a man _ brought _ to life.

(Capo 5th fret)

Intro | C | Csus4 | C | Csus2 |

Verse 1

C
I thought I saw a man brought to life.

Em
He was warm, he came around

F7
Like he was dig - nified.

He showed me what it was to cry.

C
Well, you couldn't be that man I adored.

Em
You don't seem to know, seem to care

F7
What your heart is for.

I don't know him anymore.

Am
There's nothin' where he used to lie.

G
My conversation has run dry.

Em
That's what's going on.

G   C
Nothing's fine, I'm torn.

                    C   G
Chorus 1   I'm all out of faith,

                              Am7
            This is how I feel.

                                    Fmaj7sus2
            I'm cold and I am shamed

                                  C
            Lying naked on the floor.

                              G   Am7
            Illusion never changed__ into something real.

            I'm wide awake

                Fmaj7sus2   C
            And I__ can see the perfect sky is torn.

                              G
            You're a little late,

                              Am7   Fmaj7sus2
            I'm already torn.

                C
Verse 2   So, I guess the fortune teller's right.

            Em
                I should've seen just what was there

                        F7
            And not some holy light.

            But you crawled beneath my veins, and now

            Am
            I don't care, I have no luck.

            G
                I don't miss it all that much.

            Em   G
                There's just so many things

                              C
            That I can't touch. I'm torn.

	C G
Chorus 2	I'm all out of faith,

                                      Am7
This is how I feel.

                                                     Fmaj7sus2
I'm cold and I am shamed

                           C
Lying naked on the floor.

                        G   **Am7**
Illusion never changed__ into something real.

I'm wide awake

        Fmaj7sus2   **C**
And I__ can see the perfect sky is torn.

                   G
You're a little late,

                    Am7   **Fmaj7sus2**
I'm already torn.

Am7   **Fmaj7sus2**
Torn.

	Am C G
Interlude	Oo, oo.

Verse 3
```
         Am
There's nothing where he used to lie.
G
      My inspiration has run dry.
Em
        That's what's going on.
G
        Nothing's right, I'm torn.
```

Chorus 3   ***Repeat Chorus 1***

Outro
```
                       G
I'm all out of faith,
                    Am7
This is how I feel.
                         Fmaj7sus2
I'm cold and I'm ashamed,
                          C
Bound and broken on the floor.
                   G
You're a little late.
                  Am7    Fmaj7sus2
I'm already torn.
Am7    G   Gsus4
Torn.       Oh.
| C      | G      | Am7      | Fmaj7sus2 |
```

Tropicalia

Words and Music by Beck Hansen

Melody:

Oh, when they   beat

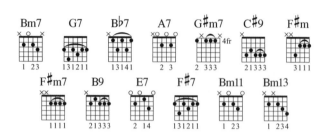

Bm7   G7   Bb7   A7   G#m7   C#9   F#m

F#m7   B9   E7   F#7   Bm11   Bm13

Intro

‖: Bm7 G7 | | Bm7 G7 | :‖

Verse 1

            Bm7   G7
Oh, when they beat upon a broken guitar,

            Bm7   G7
And all the streets, they reek of tropical charms,

            Bm7 G7
The embas-sies lie in hideous shards

         Bb7   A7
Where tourists snore and de-cay.

Verse 2

            Bm7 G7
Oh, when they dance in a reptile blaze,

            Bm7   G7   Bm7
You wear a mask, an e-quatorial haze into the past,

  G7   Bb7   A7
A colonial maze where there's no more confetti to throw.

Chorus 1

G#m7   C#9   G#m7
You wouldn't know what to say to yourself.

      C#9   F#m
Love is a poverty you couldn't sell.

F#m7 B9   E7   G7   F#7
Misery waits in vague hotels ___ to be evict-ed.

Interlude 1

| Bm7 G7 | | Bm7 G7 | |

Verse 3

     Bm7   G7
You're out of luck, you're sing-ing funeral songs

   Bm7   G7
To the studs, they're an-abolic and bronze.

     Bm7   G7
They seem to strut in their millenial fogs

   Bb7   A7
Till they ___ fall down and de-flate.

Chorus 2

Repeat Chorus 1

Interlude 2

Repeat Interlude 1

Verse 4

Bm7 G7   Bm7
Oh, and now you've had your fun

   G7   Bm7
Under an air-conditioned sun.

 G7   Bm7
It's burned into your eyes,

   G7   Bm7
Leaves you plain and left behind.

 G7   B♭7
I'll see them rise and fall

   A7   G♯m7
Into the jaws of a pestilent love.

Chorus 3

G♯m7   C♯9   G♯m7
You wouldn't know what to say to yourself.

   C♯9   F♯m
Love is a poverty you couldn't sell.

F♯m7 B9   E7 G7 F♯7
Misery waits in vague hotels ____ to be a vic-tim

Interlude 3 ‖: N.C. | :‖ *Play 8 times*

Outro   ‖: Bm7 G7 | | Bm7 G7 | :‖ *Play 4 times*
      | Bm11 | | N.C. | Bm13

Wake Up Little Susie

Words and Music by
Boudleaux Bryant and Felice Bryant

Melody:

Wake up,   lit - tle Su - sie, _

D	F/D	G/D	G	D7	A	E7	A7
132	132	132	32 4	213	123	2 1	2 3

Intro ‖: D | F/D   G/D   F/D :‖

Chorus 1

     D   F/D G/D F/D D
Wake up, little Susie, wake up.

                              F/D G/D F/D D
Wake up, little Susie, wake up.

Verse 1

        G   D7   G
We've both been sound asleep.

              D7   G
Wake up little Susie and weep.

             D7   G   D7
The movie's o - ver, it's four o-clock,

       G   D7   G
And we're in trouble deep.

Chorus 2	**A** Wake up, little Susie,

Chorus 2

        A
Wake up, little Susie,

G   **A**
  Wake up, little Susie.

                    E7   **A**
Well, what are we gonna tell your ma - ma?

              E7   **A**
What are we gonna tell your pa?

              E7   **A**
What are we gonna tell our friends

When they say, "Ooh la la?"

        A7   **D**
Wake up, ____ little Susie.

A7   **D**
  Wake up, little Susie.

Bridge

D
  Well, I told your mama that you'd be in by ten.

D7 **G**
  Well, Susie baby, looks like we goofed again.

            A
Wake up, little Susie.

G   **A**
  Wake up, little Susie.

A7 N.C.   **D**
  We gotta go home.

Interlude

‖: **D** | **F/D**   **G/D**   **F/D** :‖

Chorus 3

Repeat Chorus 1

Verse 2

      G   D7   G
The movie wasn't so hot.

           D7   G
It didn't have much of a plot.

           D7   G   D7
We fell asleep, ___ our goose is cooked,

    G   D7   G
Our reputa - tion is shot.

Chorus 4

                   A
Wake up, little Susie,

G   A
  Wake up, little Susie.

             E7   A
Well, what are we gonna tell your ma - ma?

          E7   A
What are we gonna tell your pa?

          E7   A
What are we gonna tell our friends

When they say, "Ooh la la?"

      A7   D
Wake up, ___ little Susie.

A7   D
  Wake up, little Susie.

A7   D
  Wake up, little Susie.

Outro

‖: D   F/D   G/D :‖ *Play 4 times*

‖: D | F/D   G/D   F/D :‖ *Repeat and fade*

Two Out of Three Ain't Bad

Words and Music by Jim Steinman

Melody:

Ba - by, we can talk all ___ night, ___

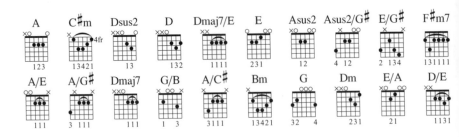

A	C#m	Dsus2
123	13421	13

D · Dmaj7/E · E · Asus2 · Asus2/G# · E/G# · F#m7
A/E · A/G# · Dmaj7 · G/B · A/C# · Bm · G · Dm · E/A · D/E

Intro | A | C#m | Dsus2 D | Dmaj7/E E |

Verse 1

Asus2   Asus2/G#
Baby, we can talk all night,

D   Dsus2   A
But that ain't getting us no - where.

          E/G#   F#m7
I told you ev'rything I possibly can,

Dmaj7/E   E
There's nothing left inside of here.

       Asus2   Asus2/G#
And maybe you can cry all night,

       D   Dsus2   A   Asus2
But that'll never change the way ___ that I feel.

A/E   A/G#   F#m7
The snow is really piling up outside,

Dmaj7   E
I wish you wouldn't make me leave here.

Pre-Chorus 1

```
D                    E        A        G/B  A/C#
I poured it on and I poured ___ it out.
D                    E        A        Bm   C#m
I tried to show you just how much I care.
D                    E        A        F#m7
I'm tired of words and I'm too hoarse to shout.
G
But you've been cold to me so long,
         D                   E
I'm crying icicles instead of tears.
         D     E    D    E
And all I can do is keep on telling you,
```

Chorus 1

```
A                    E/G#
I want you, (I want you.)
F#m7
I need you, (I need you.)
         D     E    C#m        F#m7
But there ain't no way I'm ev - er gonna love you.
         Bm
Now, don't be sad,
         D           Dm      F#m7
'Cause two outta three ___ ain't bad.
         Bm
Now, don't be sad,
         D           Dm      A    E/A  A  G/B  A/C#
'Cause two outta three ___ ain't bad.
```

Bridge

       D   E A
You'll never find your gold on a sandy beach.

  E   D   E   A
  You'll never drill for oil on a city street.

  E   D   E   A
I know you're looking for a ru-by in a mountain of rocks,

           G
But there ain't no Coupe de Ville

                  E
Hiding at the bottom of a Crackerjack box.

C♯m   D
  I can't lie, I can't tell you that I'm something I'm not.

                 C♯m
No matter how I try, I'll never be able to give you something,

D   E
Something that I just haven't got.

Verse 2

             Asus2   Asus2/G♯
Well, there's only one girl that I will ever love,

             D   Dsus2   A/E   Asus2
And that was   so many years _____ ago.

      A   A/G♯   F♯m7
And though I know I'll never get her out of my heart,

     Dmaj7/E   E
She never loved me back, ooh, ____ I know.

      Asus2   Asus2/G♯
Well, I re-member how she left me on a stormy night.

        D   Dsus2   A   Asus2
Oh, she kissed me and got out of our bed.

         A/E   A/G♯   F♯m7
And though I pleaded and I begged her not to walk out that door,

      Dmaj7   E
She packed her bags and turned right away.

        D/E   E   D/E   E   D/E   E
And she kept on telling me, she kept on telling me, she kept on telling me,

Chorus 2

A   E/G♯
I want you, (I want you.)

F♯m7
I need you, (I need you.)

     D E C♯m F♯m7
But there ain't no way I'm ev - er gonna love you.

  Bm
Now, don't be sad,

    D   Dm A
'Cause two outta three ___ ain't bad.

      C♯m
I want you, (I want you.)

F♯m7
I need you, (I need you.)

     D E C♯m F♯m7
But there ain't no way I'm ev - er gonna love you.

  Bm
Now, don't be sad,

    D   Dm F♯m7
'Cause two outta three ___ ain't bad.

  Bm
Now, don't be sad,

    D   Dm   A
'Cause two outta three ___ ain't bad.

Outro

A   N.C.
Baby, we can talk all night,

But that ain't getting us nowhere.

When the Children Cry

Words and Music by Mike Tramp and Vito Bratta

Melody:

Lit - tle child

Em   G   D/F#   Em(add9)   Bm   C

Cadd9   D   Bm7   G5/F#   Dsus4

Intro

‖: Em | | | G D/F# :‖
| Em(add9) | Bm | C Cadd9 | G D/F# |
| Em(add9) | Bm | C Cadd9 | D |

Verse 1

G   D/F♯ Em   Bm7
Little child   dry your cry - ing eyes.

C Cadd9 G   G5/F♯ Em(add9)   D
How can I ___ explain the fear you feel inside?

G   D/F♯ Em   Bm7
'Cause you were born into this evil world.

C   Cadd9 G   G5/F♯ Em(add9)   D
Where man is kill - ing man and no one knows just why.

Pre-Chorus 1

C   Bm
What have we become?

Em(add9)   Bm
Just look what we ___ have done.

C Cadd9   G   G5/F♯
All that we've ___ destroyed

Em(add9)   D Dsus4 D
You must build a-gain.

Chorus 1
       Em(add9) Bm   **C   Cadd9 G**
When the children cry ___ let them know we tried.

      G5/F♯   Em(add9)   Bm   **C Cadd9   D**
'Cause when the children sing ___ then the new world begins.

Verse 2
G   **D/F♯ Em**   **Bm7**
  Little child   you must show the way

C Cadd9 G   **G5/F♯ Em(add9) D**
  To a bet - ter day ___ for all the   young.

G   **D/F♯ Em**   **Bm7**
  'Cause you were born   for the world to see

C Cadd9   G   **G5/F♯ Em(add9)**   **D**
  That we all can live with love _____ and ___ peace.

Pre-Chorus 2
C   **Bm**
No more presidents.

Em(add9)   **Bm**
  And all the wars ___ will end.

C Cadd9 G   **G5/F♯ Em(add9)**   **D Dsus4 D**
  One unit - ed world   under God.

Chorus 2
       Em(add9) Bm   **C   Cadd9 G**
When the children cry ___ let them know we tried.

      G5/F♯ Em(add9)   Bm   **C Cadd9**   **D Dsus4 D**
'Cause when the children sing __ then the new world begins.

Guitar Solo   *Repeat Verse 1 (Instrumental)*

Pre-Chorus 3 *Repeat Pre-Chorus 1*

Pre-Chorus 4 *Repeat Pre-Chorus 2*

Chorus 3
       Em(add9) Bm   **C   Cadd9 G**
When the children cry ___ let them know we tried.

      G5/F♯ Em(add9)   Bm   **C Cadd9   D**
'Cause when the children fight ___ let them know it ain't right.

G G5/F♯ Em(add9) Bm   **C   Cadd9 G**
  When the children pray ___ let them know the way.

      G5/F♯ Em(add9)   Bm   **C Cadd9   D**
'Cause when the   children sing ___ then the new world begins.

Wherever You Will Go

Words and Music by Aaron Kamin and Alex Band

Melody:

So late - ly,

(Capo 2nd fret)

Intro

| C | Csus2/B | Am7 | F⁶₉(no3rd) | Gsus4 |

Verse 1

C   Csus2/B
So late-ly,   been wond'ring

Am7   F⁶₉(no3rd)   Gsus4
Who will be there ___ to take my ___ place.

C   Csus2/B
When I'm gone,   you'll need love

Am7   F⁶₉(no3rd)   Gsus4   C
To light the shadows on your ___ face.

     Csus2/B   Am7
If the great - er wave shall fall,

    F⁶₉(no3rd)   Gsus4 C
And fall ___ upon us ___ all,

     Csus2/B   Am7
Then between ___ the sand and stone,

     F⁶₉(no3rd)
Could you make ___ it on your own?

C   Csus2/B
If I could,   then I would,

Am7   Fsus2(maj7) C
I'll go wher-ever you will go.

Csus2/B
Way up high,   or down low,

Am7   F$^6_9$(no3rd)   Gsus4
I'll go wher-ever you will ___ go.

C   Csus2/B
And maybe   I'll find out

Am7   F$^6_9$(no3rd)   Gsus4   C
A way to make it back some ___ day.

Csus2/B
Towards you,   to guide you

Am7   F$^6_9$(no3rd)   Gsus4 C
Through the darkest of your ___ days.

Csus2/B   Am7
If the great - er wave shall fall

F$^6_9$(no3rd)   Gsus4 C
And fall ___ upon us all,

Csus2/B   Am7
Well, then I hope there's someone out ___ there who

F$^6_9$(no3rd)
Can bring me back too.

C   Csus2/B
If I could,   then I would,

Am7   Fsus2(maj7) C
I'll go wher-ever you will go.

Csus2/B
Way up high,   or down low,

Am7   Fsus2(maj7)
I'll go wher-ever you will

Bridge

Bm G   A6
Go. Run away with my heart,

F#m   Bm
Run away with my hope.

G   A6 F#m
Run away with my love.

Verse 3

C   Csus2/B
 I know now   just quite how

Am7   F⁶₉(no3rd) Gsus4 C
 My life and love ___ might still go ___ on.

      Csus2/B
In your heart, in your mind,

Am7   F⁶₉(no3rd)
 I'll stay with you for all of time.

Chorus 3

C   Csus2/B
 If I could, then I would,

Am7   Fsus2(maj7) C
 I'll go wher-ever you will go.

      Csus2/B
Way up high, or down low,

Am7   Fsus2(maj7) C
 I'll go wher-ever you will go.

    Csus2/B Am7
If I could turn back time,

    Fsus2(maj7) C
I'll go wher-ever you will go.

    Csus2/B Am7
If I could make you mine,

     Fsus2(maj7) C Csus2/B Am7
I'll go wher-ever you will go.

     Fsus2(maj7) C Csus2/B Am7 Fsus2(maj7) Fadd9
I'll go wher-ever you will go.

Wonderwall

Words and Music by Noel Gallagher

(Capo 2nd fret)

Em7   G   Dsus4   A7sus4   Cadd9   C   D   D/F#   Em11

Intro   ‖: Em7   G | Dsus4   A7sus4   :‖   *Play 4 times*

Verse 1

Em7   G
Today is gon-na be the day
        Dsus4   A7sus4
That they're gonna throw it back to you.
Em7   G
By now you should have somehow
    Dsus4   A7sus4
Real-ized what you gotta do.
Em7   G
I don't believe that an - ybody
Dsus4   A7sus4   Cadd9 Dsus4 A7sus4
Feels the way I do about you now.

Verse 2

Em7   G
Backbeat, the word is on the street
        Dsus4   A7sus4
That the fire in your heart is out.
Em7   G
I'm sure you've heard it all before,
        Dsus4   A7sus4
But you never really had a doubt.
Em7   G
I don't believe that an-ybody
Dsus4   A7sus4   Em7 G Dsus4 A7sus4
Feels the way I do about you now.

ACOUSTIC ROCK

Chorus 1

      C   D   Em7

And all ___ the roads we have ___ to walk are wind - ing,

      C   D   Em7

And all ___ the lights that lead ___ us there are blind - ing.

C   D

There are many things ___ that I would

G   D/F♯   Em7   G   A7sus4

Like to say to you, ___ but I don't know how.

         Cadd9 Em7 G   Em7

Because maybe _____ you're gon-na

            Cadd9   Em7   G

Be the one that saves me.

       Em7 Cadd9 Em7 G   Em7   Cadd9   Em7

And af - ter all _____ you're my wonderwall.

| G   Em7 | | Em11 |

Verse 3

Em7   G

   Today was gon-na be the day,

   Dsus4   A7sus4

But they'll never throw it back to you.

Em7   G

   By now you should have somehow

   Dsus4   A7sus4

Real-ized what you're not to do.

Em7   G

I don't believe that an-ybody

Dsus4   A7sus4   Em7   G   Dsus4 A7sus4

Feels the way I do about you now.

Chorus 2

          C   **D**   **Em7**
And all ___ the roads that lead ___ you there were wind - ing,

         C   **D**   **Em7**
And all ___ the lights that light ___ the way are blind - ing.

C   **D**
There are many things ___ that I would

G **D/F♯**   **Em7**   **G**   **A7sus4**
Like to say to you, ___ but I don't know how.

       Cadd9 **Em7** **G**   **Em7**
I said maybe _____ you're gon-na

            Cadd9 **Em7**   **G**
Be the one that saves me.

      Em7 **Cadd9** **Em7** **G**
And af - ter all

         Em7   **Cadd9**   **Em7**   **G**   **Em7**
You're my wonderwall.

       Cadd9 **Em7** **G**   **Em7**
I said maybe _____ you're gon-na

            Cadd9 **Em7** **G**
Be the one that saves me.

      Em7 **Cadd9**   **Em7**   **G**
And af - ter all

        Em7   **Cadd9** **Em7** **G** **Em7**
You're my won - derwall.

       Cadd9 **Em7** **G**   **Em7**
I said maybe _____ you're gon-na

           Cadd9 **Em7** **G**
Be the one that saves me.

       Em7   **Cadd9** **Em7** **G**
You're gon-na be the one that saves me.

       Em7   **Cadd9** **Em7** **G** **Em7**
You're gon-na be the one that saves me.

Outro   ‖: **Cadd9**   **Em7** | **G**   **Em7**   :‖ *Play 3 times*
             | **Cadd9**   **Em7** | **G**   **Em7**

Yellow

Words and Music by Guy Berryman,
Jon Buckland, Will Champion and Chris Martin

Tuning:
(low to high) E–A–B–G–B–D#

Melody:

Look at the stars,

B   Badd11   F#6   Emaj7   G#m   Eadd9   B*   F#m11

Intro

B		Badd11	B		Badd11
B		Badd11	F#6		
Emaj7			B		Badd11

Verse 1

B   F#6
   Look at the stars, look how they shine for ___ you,

         Emaj7
And ev'rything you do, ___ yeah, they were all yellow.

B   F#6
   I came along, I wrote a song for ___ you,

             Emaj7   B
And all the things you do, ___ and it was called yellow.

Badd11   F#6
   So then I took my ___ turn,

          Emaj7
Oh, what a thing to've done,

        B   Badd11   B
And it was all yellow.

Emaj7   G#m   F#6   Emaj7
   Your skin, ___ oh yeah, your skin and bones,

     G#m   F#6
Turn in - to some-thing beautiful.

Emaj7   G#m   F#6   Emaj7
   And you know, ___ you know I love you so,

Eadd9
   You know I love you so.

| Interlude 1 | <code>|B | |F#6 | |</code> |

<code>|Emaj7 | |B | |</code>

Verse 2

B   F#6

    I swam across, I jumped across for ____ you,

                         Emaj7

Oh, what a thing to do, ____ 'cause you were all yellow.

B   Badd11   F#6

    I drew a line, I drew a line for ____ you,

                 Emaj7   B   Badd11   B

Oh, what a thing to do, ____ and it was all yellow.

Emaj7   G#m   F#6   Emaj7

Your skin, ____ oh yeah, your skin and bones,

     G#m   F#6

Turn in - to some-thing beautiful.

Emaj7   G#m   F#6   Emaj7

And you know, ____ for you I'd bleed myself dry,

Eadd9   B

For you I'd bleed myself dry.

Interlude 2   *Repeat Interlude 1*

Chorus

      B   F#6

It's true, look how they shine for you,

                Emaj7

Look how they shine for you,

            B

Look how they shine for,

           F#6

Look how they shine for you,

            Emaj7

Look how they shine for you,

Look how they shine.

Outro

B*

    Look at the stars,

              F#m11

Look how they shine for ____ you,

             Emaj7

And all the things that you ____ do.

Yesterday

Words and Music by
John Lennon and
Paul McCartney

Melody:

Yes-ter day,   all my trou-bles seemed so far a-way.

Tune down 1 step:
(low to high) D-G-C-F-A-D

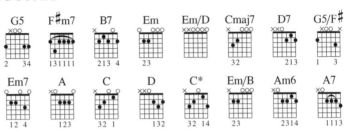

G5   F#m7   B7   Em   Em/D   Cmaj7   D7   G5/F#

Em7   A   C   D   C*   Em/B   Am6   A7

Intro

| G5 | | |

Verse 1

G5   F#m7
Yesterday,

    B7   Em   Em/D
All my troubles seemed so far away.

Cmaj7 D7   G5   G5/F#
  Now it looks as though they're here to stay.

    Em7   A   C   G5
Oh, I believe___ in yes - terday.

Verse 2

G5   F#m7
Suddenly,

    B7   Em   Em/D
I'm not half the man I used to be.

Cmaj7   D7   G5   G5/F#
  There's a shad - ow hanging over me,

    Em7   A   C   G5
Oh, yesterday___ came sud - denly.

Bridge 1

F#m7 B7 Em D C*
Why she had to go

Em/B Am6 D7 G5
I don't know, she wouldn't say.

F#m7 B7 Em D C*
I said some-thing wrong.

Em/B Am6 D7 G5
Now I___ long for yester-day.

Verse 3

G5 F#m7
Yesterday,

B7 Em Em/D
Love was such an easy game to play.

Cmaj7 D7 G5 G5/F#
Now I need a place to hide away.

Em7 A C G5
Oh, I believe___ in yes - terday.

Bridge 2

Repeat Bridge 1

Verse 4

G5 F#m7
Yesterday,

B7 Em Em/D
Love was such an easy game to play.

Cmaj7 D7 G5 G5/F#
Now I need a place to hide away.

Em7 A C G5
Oh, I believe___ in yes - terday.

G A7 C* G5
Mm.

You've Got a Friend

Words and Music by Carole King

Melody:

When you're   down___   and trou - bled,

(Capo 2nd fret)

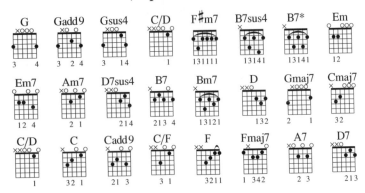

Intro | G Gadd9 Gsus4| C/D | Gsus4 G Gadd9 G| F#m7 B7sus4

Verse 1

      B7*   Em   B7
When you're down___ and trou - bled,

      Em   B7   Em Em7
And you need a helping hand,

      Am7   D7sus4   G Gsus4 G Gsus4 G
And nothing, whoa, nothing is goin' right,

F#m7   B7
Close your eyes and think of me,

      Em   B7   Em Em7
And soon I will___ be there

      Am7   Bm7   D7sus4   D
To brighten up even your darkest night.

GUITAR CHORD SONGBOO

Chorus 1

         G   Gmaj7
You just call__ out my name,

      Cmaj7   Am7
And you know wherever I am

D7sus4   G   Gmaj7
I'll come run - ning, oh yeah, babe,

               D7sus4
To see you again.

G   Gmaj7
Winter, spring, summer or fall,

     Cmaj7   Em7
Now, all you got to do is call,

       Cmaj7 Bm7   C/D D7sus4
And I'll be there,__ yeah, yeah, yeah.

               G Gadd9 G C   G   F#m7 B7sus4
You've got a friend.

Verse 2

     B7   Em   B7
If the sky__ above__ you

        Em   B7   Em Em7
Should turn__ dark and full of clouds,

       Am7   D7sus4   G Gsus4 G
And that old North wind should begin to blow,

F#m7   B7
   Keep your head togeth - er

     Em   B7   Em Em7   Am7
And call my name__ out loud, now.

         Bm7   D7sus4
Soon I'll be knock - in' upon your door.

Chorus 2

Cadd9   Gmaj7
You just call__ out my name,

      Cmaj7   Am7
And you know__ wherever I am,

D7sus4 G Gsus4   G
I'll come run - ning,   oh yes, I will,

              D7sus4
To see you again.

G   Gmaj7
Winter, spring, summer or fall,

    Cmaj7   Em7
Yeah, all you got to do is call,

         Cmaj7   Bm7   C/D D7sus4
And I'll be there, yeah,__ yeah, yeah.

Bridge

         C/F   F
Hey, ain't__ it good to know

    C/D
That you've got a friend

      G   Gsus4   Gmaj7
When people can be__ so cold?

      C
They'll hurt you,

      Fmaj7
And desert you.

        Em   Em7   A7
Well, they'll take your soul if you let__ them,

           D7sus4   D7
Oh yeah, but don't__ you let them.

Chorus 3
    Gmaj7
You just call__ out my name,

    Cmaj7   **Am7**
And you know wherever I am,

D7sus4   **G**   **Gsus4**   **G**
  I'll come run-ning

           D7sus4
To see you again.

Oh, babe, don't you know 'bout

G   **Gmaj7**
Winter, spring, summer or fall,

    Cmaj7   **Em7**
Hey, now all you've got to do is call.

      Cmaj7   **Bm7**   **C/D** **D7sus4**
Lord, I'll be__ there, yes, I will.

            G **Gadd9 G** **C**
Outro   You've got a friend.

           G
You've got a friend, yeah.

C   **G**
  Ain't it good to know you've got__ a friend?

    C
Ain't it good to know

          Gsus4 **G** **Gadd9** **G**
You've got a friend?

    C   **Gsus4** **G** **Gadd9** **G**
Oh,__ yeah, yeah. You've got a friend.

'39

Words and Music by Brian May

Tune up 1/2 step:
(low to high) F–Bb–Eb–Ab–C–F

Melody:

In the year __ of thir-ty-nine, __ as-sem-bled here __

C | Am | E | Bb/F | Eb | Bb | Csus4 | F | G5
G/B | D | Dsus2 | Em | C* | G | Dsus4 | Cmaj7 | Em7/D
D#°7 | Am* | B7 | Eb* | Ebadd#4 | Eb6 | Cm | A | F#m

Intro

C		Am	E
Bb/F	Eb Bb Csus4 F	G5	
G/B D Dsus2 D	Em C*	G D Dsus2 D	
C* G	G/B Dsus4 D	Em C* Cmaj7	
	G		

Verse 1

                D   **Em**
In the year ___ of thirty-nine, assembled here ___ the volunteers,

                C*   **G**   **D**
In the days ___ when the lands ___ were few.

           Em   **Em7/D**   **C***   **Cmaj7**
Here the ship sailed out ___ into the blue ___ and sunny morn.

Dsus4 **D**   **G**
Sweetest sight ever seen.

           D   **D#°7**
And the night followed day, and the storytellers say,

        Em   **Am***
That the score brave souls inside.

        G   **D**   **G**
Mmm, for many a lonely day sailed across ___ the milky seas.

C*   **Em** **C***   **D G C***   **D**
Ne'er looked back, never feared, _____ never cried.

GUITAR CHORD SONGBOOK

Chorus 1

    G
(Don't you hear my call?)

       C*
Though you're many years away.

      G   D
(Don't you hear me callin' you?)

      G   B7   Em
Write your letters in the sand,

   G   C*   G   Am*
For ___ the day ___ I take ___ your hand

     G/B C*   D   G
In the land that our grandchildren knew.

Interlude

E♭* E♭add♯4 E♭*	E♭6 E♭*	
Cm		A	
C	F♯m C	Am	E
B♭/F	E♭ B♭ Csus4 F	G	

Verse 2

        D   Em   C*
In the year ___ of '39, came a ship ___ in from the blue.

           G   D
The volunteers ___ came home that day.

      Em   Em7/D   C*   Cmaj7
And they bring good news ___ of a world ___ so newly born,

Dsus4   D   G
Though their hearts so heavily weigh.

        D   D♯ 7
For the earth is old and grey, little darlin', we'll away,

Em   Am*
But my love, this cannot be.

        G   D   G
Oh, so many years have gone, though I'm older but ___ a year.

C*   Em C*   D G C*   D
Your mother's eyes, from your eyes, _____ cry to me.

Chorus 2

       G
(Don't you hear my call?)

       C*
Though you're many years away.

      G   **D**
(Don't you hear me callin' you?)

      G **B7** **Em**
Write your letters in the sand,

   G   **C***   **G**   **Am***
For ___ the day ___ I take ___ your hand

    G/B C   **D**   **G**   **D**
In the land that our grandchildren knew.

      G   **C***
(Don't you hear my call though you're many years away?)

      G   **D**
(Don't you hear me callin' you?)

    G **B7** **Em**
All your letters in the sand

   G   **C*** **G**   **Am***
Can-not heal ___ me like your hand.

    Em   **D**
For my life still a-head, pity me.

Outro | **G**   **D** | **E** **C** **Cmaj7** | **D** | **G**   **G5**

uitar Chord Songbooks

Each book includes complete lyrics, chord symbols, and guitar chord diagrams.

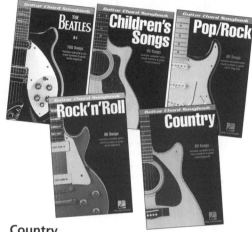

Beatles (A-I)
some reference of 100 Beatles hits, including: All My
• All You Need Is Love • Back in the U.S.S.R. • Can't
e Love • Eleanor Rigby • Get Back • A Hard Day's
Hey Jude • In My Life • and more.
558 . . . .$16.95

Beatles (J-Y)
ore Beatles hits, including: Lady Madonna • Let It Be
Long and Winding Road • Love Me Do • Michelle •
ion • Sgt. Pepper's Lonely Hearts Club Band • She
You • Twist and Shout • When I'm Sixty-Four •
ay • and more.
62 . . . .$16.95

ren's Songs
songs for kids, including: Alphabet Song • Any Dream
• The Brady Bunch • The Candy Man • Do-Re-Mi •
ss • It's a Small World • Puff the Magic Dragon • The
/ Connection • Sing • Supercalifragilisticexpialidocious
Me Out to the Ball Game • and more!
39 . . . .$12.95

tmas Carols
nient reference of 80 Christmas carols, include: Angels
Heard on High • Away in a Manger • Deck the Hall •
ng Wenceslas • The Holly and the Ivy • Jingle Bells •
ie World • O Holy Night • Silent Night • Up on the
p • What Child Is This? • and more.
36 . . . .$12.95

tmas Songs
mas favorites, including: Baby, It's Cold Outside • The
k Song • The Christmas Shoes • The Christmas Song
ts Roasting on an Open Fire) • Feliz Navidad • Frosty
Man • I've Got My Love to Keep Me Warm • Rudolph
Nosed Reindeer • Silver Bells • We Need a Little
s • What Are You Doing New Year's Eve? • and more.
7 . . . .$12.95

lapton
whand's best, including: Badge • Bell Bottom Blues
e • I Can't Stand It • I Shot the Sheriff • Lay Down
Layla • Riding with the King • Strange Brew •
of Your Love • Tears in Heaven • White Room •
il Tonight • and more.
7 . . . .$14.95

mporary Christian
asy-to-use collection of just the chords and lyrics to
om today's top CCM artists. Includes: Abba (Father)
Awesome God • Don't Look at Me • El Shaddai •
aithful • Friends • The Great Divide • He Will Carry
s Strength Is Perfect • I Will Be Here • Just One •
Loud • Love Will Be Our Home • A Maze of Grace
rd, You're Beautiful • Pray • Run to You •
ss • Testify to Love • Via Dolorosa • and more.
. . . .$14.95

Country
80 country standards, including: Abilene • Always on My Mind
• Amazed • Blue • Boot Scootin' Boogie • Breathe • Could I
Have This Dance • Crazy • Folsom Prison Blues • Friends in
Low Places • Hey, Good Lookin' • I Feel Lucky • I Hope You
Dance • Sixteen Tons • Your Cheatin' Heart • and more.
00699534 . . . .$12.95

Folksongs
80 folk favorites, including: Aura Lee • Camptown Races •
Deep River • Git Along, Little Dogies • Home on the Range •
Hush, Little Baby • Man of Constant Sorrow • Nobody Knows
the Trouble I've Seen • Scarborough Fair • When the Saints
Go Marching In • and more.
00699541 . . . .$12.95

Pop/Rock
The chords and lyrics to 80 chart hits, including: All I Wanna
Do • Closer to Free • Come Sail Away • Drops of Jupiter
(Tell Me) • Every Breath You Take • Give a Little Bit •
Heartache Tonight • I Will Remember You • Imagine • More
Than Words • Mr. Jones • Smooth • Summer of '69 •
Superman (It's Not Easy) • Time After Time • What I Like
About You • Wonderful Tonight • and more.
00699538 . . . .$14.95

Rock 'n' Roll
80 rock 'n' roll classics in one convenient collection: All
Shook Up • At the Hop • Blue Suede Shoes • Chantilly Lace •
Duke of Earl • Great Balls of Fire • It's My Party • La Bamba
• The Loco-Motion • My Boyfriend's Back • Peggy Sue • Rock
Around the Clock • Stand by Me • Surfin' U.S.A. • and more.
00699535 . . . .$12.95

FOR MORE INFORMATION, SEE YOUR LOCAL MUSIC DEALER,
OR WRITE TO:

HAL•LEONARD®
CORPORATION
7777 W. BLUEMOUND RD. P.O. BOX 13819 MILWAUKEE, WI 53213

Visit Hal Leonard online at **www.halleonard.com**
Prices, contents, and availability subject to change without notice.

0404

HAL LEONARD GUITAR METHO

This comprehensive method is preferred by teachers and students alike for many reasons:
- Learning sequence is carefully paced with clear instructions that make it easy to learn.
- Popular songs increase the incentive to learn to play. • Versatile enough to be used as self-instruction or with a teacher. • CD accompaniments let students have fun and sound great while practicing.

METHOD BOOKS

BOOK 1

Book 1 provides beginning instruction which covers: tuning; playing position; musical symbols; notes in first position; the C, G, G7, D, D7, A7 and Em chords; rhythms through eighth notes; strumming and picking; 100 great songs; riffs and examples. Added features are a chord chart and a selection of well-known songs, including "Ode to Joy," "Rockin' Robin," "Give My Regards to Broadway," and "Time Is on My Side."

00699010 Book $5.95
00699027 Book/CD Pack $9.95

BOOK 2

Book 2 continues the instruction started in Book 1 and covers: Am, Dm, A, E, F and B7 chords; power chords; finger-style guitar; syncopations, dotted rhythms, and triplets; Carter-style solos; bass runs; pentatonic scales; improvising; tablature; 92 great songs, riffs and examples; notes in first and second position; and more!

00699020 Book $5.95
00697313 Book/CD Pack $9.95

BOOK 3

Book 3 covers: the major, minor, pentatonic and chromatic sixteenth notes; barre chords; drop D tuning; movable scales; fifth position; slides, hammer-ons, pull-offs and string bends construction; gear; 90 great songs, riffs and examples; and me CD includes 61 full-band tracks for demonstration or play-alo

00699030 Book . . . .
00697316 Book/CD Pack . . . .

COMPOSITE

Books 1, 2, and 3 bound together in an easy-to-use spiral bir

00699040 Book . . . .
00697342 Book/CD . . . .

HAL LEONARD GUITAR METHOD DVD

For the beginning electric or acoustic guitarist

00697318 DVD . . . .

SONGBOOKS

EASY POP RHYTHMS

00697336 Book $5.95
00697309 Book/CD Pack $14.95

MORE EASY POP RHYTHMS

00697338 Book $5.95
00697322 Book/CD Pack $14.95

EVEN MORE EASY POP RHYTHMS

00697340 Book $5.95
00697323 Book/CD Pack $14.95

EASY POP MELODIES

00697281 Book . . . .
00697268 Book/CD Pack . . . .

MORE EASY POP MELODIES

00697280 Book . . . .
00697269 Book/CD Pack . . . .

EVEN MORE EASY POP MELODIES

00699154 Book . . . .
00697270 Book/CD Pack . . . .

SUPPLEMENTAL REFERENCE

ARPEGGIO FINDER

00697351 9" x 12" $5.95
00697352 6" x 9" $4.95

INCREDIBLE CHORD FINDER

00697209 9" x 12" $5.95
00697200 6" x 9" $4.95

INCREDIBLE SCALE FINDER

00695490 9" x 12" . . . .
00695568 6" x 9" . . . .

STYLISTIC METHODS

BLUES GUITAR

by Greg Koch

00697326 9" x 12" Book/CD Pack $12.95
00697344 6" x 9" Book/CD Pack $12.95

COUNTRY GUITAR

by Greg Koch

00697337 9" x 12" Book/CD Pack $12.95

JAZZ GUITAR

by Jeff Schroedl

00695359 9" x 12" Book/CD Pack . . . .

ROCK GUITAR

by Michael Mueller

00697319 9" x 12" Book/CD Pack . . . .
00697343 6" x 9" Book/CD Pack . . . .

Visit Hal Leonard Online at
www.halleonard.com

Prices, contents and availability subject to change without notic